FOR LOVE OF THE WORLD

FOR LOVE OF THE WORLD

A Harangue with Practical Guidance on Writing and Performing Solo Dramas That Matter

Deborah Lubar

HEINEMANN
Portsmouth, NH

Heinemann
A division of Reed Elsevier Inc.
361 Hanover Street
Portsmouth, NH 03801–3912
www.heinemanndrama.com

Offices and agents throughout the world

The author and publisher wish to thank those who have generously given permission to reprint borrowed material:

Excerpts adapted from *Hands of Light* by Barbara Ann Brennan. Copyright © 1987 by Barbara Ann Brennan. Used by permission of Bantam Books, a division of Random House, Inc.

Excerpts adapted from *Light Emerging* by Barbara Ann Brennan. Copyright © 1993 by Barbara Ann Brennan. Used by permission of Bantam Books, a division of Random House, Inc.

Library of Congress Cataloging-in-Publication Data
Lubar, Deborah.
    For love of the world : a harangue with practical guidance on writing and performing solo dramas that matter / by Deborah Lubar.
    p. cm.
    Includes bibliographical references.
    ISBN-13: 978-0-325-00839-4
    ISBN-10: 0-325-00839-6 1. Monologue I. Title.
    PN1530.L83 2007
    792.02′8—dc22   2006038189

Editors: Lisa A. Barnett and Danny Miller
Production service: Matrix Productions, Inc.
Production supervisor: Patricia Adams
Typesetter: TechBooks
Cover design: Joni Doherty
Inside Illustrator: Janet Fredericks
Manufacturing: Steve Bernier

Printed in the United States of America on acid-free paper
11 10 09 08 07 VP 1 2 3 4 5

For my goddaughter, Abigail Nessen,
and the young ones like her of fierce, lit talent and spirit,
who love the world as much as they love their art.

CONTENTS

ACKNOWLEDGMENTS

I thank with all my heart more people than I can list here, but especially all the teachers who know they've been my teachers; and Martín Prechtel, who has taught me more about Beauty than all the others piled up together, even though he would roll his eyes and wrinkle his nose at some of what's in this book. I also thank all the teachers who had no idea they've been my teachers: those brave people from many lands whose sparked stories I've been blessed to hear and grow from, and those whose books and poems have been lighting my way since I was little, all of you changing my life over and over again.

Special thanks is due to Janet Fredericks for her illustrations and generosity; Len Berkman, who in his inimitable way helped jump-start the engine of publication; and Bernie Lubarsky for his crazy but doggedly persistent ways of handing down his love and respect for words, theatre, and music.

I thank my two magnificent editors at Heinemann: Lisa Barnett—whose untimely death came before the book was done and who is mourned by all who knew her. I am forever grateful for her kindness, intelligence, support, and patience from the beginning. And Danny Miller, who took over at a critical juncture. I bow to you for your indispensable help so steadily and generously laced with wisdom, humor, your penetrating eye and integrity, plus it turns out you were right about pretty much everything.

Last, I thank Marianne Lust for far too many things to list (I do have a word limit), but her enduring support in a hundred ways throughout the writing of this book and her blazingly intelligent criticism of the text are no small part of it.

For Love of the World

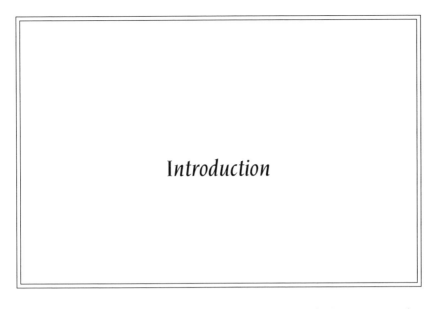

Introduction

There is too much cold in the world now, and it has worked its way into the hearts of all living creatures and down into the roots of the grass and the trees.
—Chan K'in Viejo

Either we have hope or we don't; it's a dimension of the soul. it's an orientation of the heart. . . . Only by looking outward, . . . by throwing oneself over and over into the tumult of this world with the intention of making one's voice count—only thus does one really become a person, a creator of "the order of the spirit," a being capable of a miracle: the recreation of the world.
—Vaclav Havel

LOOKING FOR SPARKS

This is a book for American dramatists and actors with some solid training already under their belts, who sense in their bones what is cold and broken in our times as well as what's magnificent, and who are lit with that "orientation of the heart" of which Havel speaks. It began especially for the young ones as they set forth in their extravagantly imaginative ways to reinvigorate our theatre's blood cells. But in the end it's for those of any age who, compelled "to look outward and throw themselves into the tumult of this world," are drawn to the possibility of theatre as a way of singing to and nourishing a world at the edge, and as a fire to warm the windy places where too much cold has worked its way.

I find many artists now, both young and older, looking clear-eyed at the hungers and the turmoil of our world and then at their options in theatre, wondering, *Why not be a social worker, a human rights lawyer, a doctor without borders, a teacher in the inner city, an environmentalist, an activist . . . What on God's earth am I doing prancing about in glitzy costumes on a stage?* Even knowing the traditional ways in which live theatre can be valuable, meaningful, and uplifting, they're asking more. With what intention do we wish to bring people together for a performance? And in what manner? And with what gift of perceiving and reflecting our world? What risks are we willing to take in our own lives to find the hidden flames which might light the way and strengthen our steps across the rough and unstable terrain of our times?

Part reflection, part practice, *For Love of the World* looks at these questions in relation to our creating solo dramas for this particular world at this particular time, finding the stories to inspire them, and nurturing a quality of heart and spirit to spark both the gathering and embodying of such stories. The reflection part includes explanation, suggestion, advice, and a little haranguing. The practice is inspired for the most part by elements of what's called "spiritual healing," in particular theories and techniques having to do with invisible force fields of energy which surround and permeate our physical bodies. If this sounds a bit odd, "out there," or mystifying, be assured that there is lengthy explanation later, along with an examination of how a grasp of the nature and workings of these "energy fields" applies directly, concretely, and usefully to our work in theatre. You'll find exercises in many of the chapters, most having to do with these energetic force fields, as well as some practices to be explored anytime and anywhere, called *arpeggios*.

Why monologue? Not because it has more inherent merit than other forms of drama, but simply because it's what I do, what I know best, and what I've experienced to be an exquisitely valuable dramatic form. Although the term "solo drama" is used in the title to distinguish this book from those concerning audition monologues and short dramatic speeches, I use "monologue" throughout the text to mean two possibilities: either one person on stage for a full evening's performance, or, when it serves, two or more actors in the production, each performing solo speeches related to one another thematically but not in conventional dialogue form.

In both cases, the structure is built from monologues. And whether performed solo or with more than one actor, there's a fundamental simplicity to the construct that has good things going for it in a spare and unglamorous kind of way:

It's inexpensive.

It's bare-boned and low-tech.

It travels easily and can cavort in small spaces.

It engenders an unusually direct and intimate relationship with an audience.

Yet, while cheap, small, and spare, dramatic monologue provides luxurious room for deeply nuanced character portrayal—enough space for the Byzantine mazes, twisted and shadowed alleys, secret gardens, and sun-glanced courtyards of our human psyche and soul.

There are, of course, countless stories which lend themselves well to drama, but a particular kind is suggested here as the pulse of and impulse for monologue in our current times. In these chapters there is guidance on finding the heartbeat of such stories, on gathering and transmuting them into drama, on enriching and enlivening the spirit of the characters who speak them, and some thoughts about why we need to hear them in the first place. The emphasis is not on traditional tales—as in folk tale, fairy tale, and myth—but on those stories of human experience that are more often than not hidden, lost, dismissed, unheard, or swept under the carpet of our ignorance or apathy; the unsung and unconsidered stories of individuals and cultures which thread by thread and woven together into rich tapestries, reveal a more refined and capacious view of our Larger Human Story than what we're usually offered in the daily tales of our fractured world. Stories that expose our being—as a culture, as a species, as a world—at the crux of a critical crossroads, with many of us feeling we have lost our way and searching for a new and redemptive road, the old one no longer viable.

I suppose you could say such a thing about a hundred other periods of history, but this time, given technology's power and the global sweep of things both good and bad, we seem balanced on a sharper edge, the stakes higher. There are said to be gods of such crossroads; perhaps they sit—dressed in feathers and gold—on the tongues of these stories, and call to us through the tangled noise of our lives to remember who we really are, that we might animate our spiritual muscle for the long, slow swim against our culture's soul-smashing current of forgetfulness.

So the discussion begins with what kind of stories bear witness to the aching realities and mysteries of our humanity as it walks the world in all its shapes, colors, and styles. What kind of stories hold our lives in their tough and wiry arms, whether we know it or not, and might warm rather than freeze our blood as we look out at the broken, suffering landscapes of our world today? These bearing-witness stories need *us* to bear witness to *them*.

Bearing witness is not standing still and watching. It actually requires copious energy from within and without. Think of "bearing" as in "carrying," "supporting," or even "birthing,"—bearing gifts, bearing burdens, bearing truth, bearing life, bearing all the wild complexity of our time's exquisite possibilities and breathtaking destructiveness.

The idea of our world as wounded or broken is an old one. Ancient tales from many traditions speak of an original wholeness shattered. In an African story the bright lantern which brought the first light to all the world is dropped, smashing that clarity into thousands of small glimmers after which, as each person finds one tiny bit of light in the darkness, he believes—as many always have and many still do—that he possesses the whole.

Another such legend from the Jewish mystical tradition is told here through the loud mouth of a character in a monologue called "A Story's a Story."[1]

[Enter ROSE SOLOMON, an old Yiddish lady who emigrated from Poland to the Lower East Side at the turn of the century. She's not just old, she's dead. But from time to time she returns to earth from heaven, where she has a small but sunny apartment, to tell us some stories to perk us up in troubled times. She wears a chunky sealskin jacket over a bright polyester dress, five pounds of costume jewelry, uneven rouge, 3/4 cup of lipstick, and an orange hat with big cloth flowers. She sits with stiff-jointed difficulty, sets down her patent leather purse, and stares at the audience.

---

[1]Lubar, Deborah. 1994. "A Story's a Story," pp. 1–3.

ROSE speaks in a loud, no-nonsense voice, with a thick-like-lumpy-gravy Yiddish accent.]

ROSE

So I'll begin with a story handed over to me by my mother. It was the only story she ever told me, but she told it five hundred times.

So once upon a time, there was no world. There was just God, you see, and God's consciousness, which was so big you can't even get a handle on it. There was no form, you see. Animals weren't running around. There was no rivers. We weren't here. There was no toilets or onions. There wasn't even a lipstick, a magazine. Nothing.

So in order to create the material world, God had to contract His consciousness—like I don't know, like He took His essence, and He folded it in to make room for the other things to appear, and space that they should know they were there, and variety that we should know who we were. You know, like you're an anteater, and you're over there, and I'm not there, so this must be me over here. Ya, there's a certain kind of a logic to it.

So at this time, everything was in a state of complete divine harmony and wholeness. And in order to keep it that way, what God did, He made some vessels, and He put into them His shining essence and light, and He sent them out into the world. Now don't ask me what these vessels looked like—who knows? Maybe like miniature flying saucers—I don't know. I wasn't there, so leave me alone.

The important thing was this: A terrible thing happened, a catastrophe. These vessels, what were filled with God's shining radiance and light—they exploded. They completely shattered. We don't know, maybe because God's energy was so intense they couldn't contain it. But when these vessels broke, two things happened. Number one, the sparks of God's light escaped and scattered all around the world, hiding themselves in all kinds of things—here, there, everywhere. And number two, because these sparks of light had escaped and separated from their Source, the divine wholeness was broken, and evil and misery jumped up and spread themselves around the world.

So!—my mother continued—it is the task of all human beings to put the pieces of this broken world back together, to find these sparks and gather them up, until we have enough we should return to God and return to this state of magnificent oneness. Do you understand what I'm telling to you, Rosie?

And to sink her point in deeper, she would give me a LOOK—I can't describe it, but such a LOOK . . . I would stop whatever I was doing. I knew my main project was to find these sparks.

So I would say, "Mama, Mama, where do I begin? What size are they, what color do they have, is there a shape I should look for . . . ?"

But she would only say, "Rosie, Shh, shh! Go out into the barn and feed the chickens. Don't get lazy."

So this was the whole and only story my mother ever told me. She was a woman of few words, you see, but when she talked, you listened.

Built into the weave of this tale is the special task given to us humans of searching for the broken pieces of holiness, wherever on earth they may be hiding, and reclaiming them to mend the "broken world." In Hebrew the finding and gathering of the scattered sparks of light is called *tikkun olam:* "the repair, or making whole, of the world." Of course it may well be that the world is not broken at all, but the lenses through which we see, experience, and relate to it are smashed, and the light of the sparks might possibly restore our ability to perceive the connections, even communion, that has been there all along. Either way, we look for sparks, which can be anywhere, but often they hide inside the blood and bone of human story.

We've not been hearing enough spark-filled stories, not for a long time. They are potent tonic for thirsty souls. The most nourishing of them often grow out of a dank humus of pain, loss, and conflict; in pushing up from that harsh soil, some sprout into living shoots of resilience, defiance, courage, wisdom, vision, and thank-god humor.

QUESTIONS AND ANSWERS

After September 11, 2001, a national soul-searching arose about the role of the arts in confronting and responding to the terrorist attacks and the suddenly uncharted, anxiety-filled times in which we found ourselves. Headlines under photos of dark, forbidding clouds cried, "Artists Look into the Unknown." New artistic perspectives and approaches were sought to address "a murky and uncertain future."

Long before those terrorist attacks, of course, there had been artists of all kinds persistently and meaningfully doing just that, artists considering through their work the 20th century from which we'd just emerged—which has been called "the most indiscriminately savage century in recorded history"—and exploring ways to express and respond to the dreadful litany of human-caused disasters. Most of us can name the novelists, poets, visual artists, filmmakers, and nonfiction writers who've been tackling our "murky and uncertain future" with grace, passion, and insight; but interestingly, the work of many American theatre artists who've been confronting the issues head-on and heart-on has flown beneath the proverbial radar screen of mainstream consciousness. There are, of course, some well-known honored ones, like August Wilson, whose ten-play cycle speaks eloquently to a century of African Americans' own consistently murky and uncertain future in this country. But most others are not generally acknowledged, much less supported or honored. A storyteller works with Romanian orphans and street children in India, teaching them tales of redemption and strength. Grassroots theatres gather stories of folks in a given area—Appalachia, the Bronx, the streets of L.A.—and offer people of a particular place a chance to speak and be heard, maybe even understood. Theatre professionals go to places of war and unrest—Africa, Israel/Palestine, southeast Asia, the Mexican–U.S. border—and create theatre with those there to help heal broken lives, broken communities, and broken trust among bloody factions—hard and painstaking work. But strangely, in our mainstream theatre world, the once-urgent dialogue is rarely heard now, and things are jogging along again in their usual way as if nothing in the world were out of joint or crying out for our long-term attention and heart.

At the start of the national dialogue spurred by 9/11, one dramatist quoted in the *New York Times* concluded soberly that the central role of the theatre artist now is "to probe the depths of the human soul." At first I was stopped in my tracks by that statement with an angry, snitty response: "Oh *really*? What a remarkable concept! Was this very thing not supposed to have been our mandate for a few thousand years?!" But I got my comeuppance. After two years of following the ongoing discussion wherever I could find it, I realized one day that out of it all, only that one suggestion, that one phrase, had stayed with me. I had forgotten who'd had the courage to say it, and to say it so simply, unabashedly, and—unlike me—with the grace to spare us a tirade on whether or not we've been faithful to our longtime mandate. But I remembered the words. And I came to understand that being reminded again and again that we in theatre have the privilege and the responsibility of "probing the depths of the human soul," even though our art will never be able wholly to accomplish such a task, does not hurt. Especially in our current culture where such things as "probing" and "depth" and "soul" are not at the top of the national agenda.

The great questioning among artists that began in 2001, that sense of our being catapulted toward one another in a meaningful, collective, public conversation, has dimmed, even disappeared. It's not even clear what was craved from those in the arts. Solace? Comprehension? A momentary shape to address chaos? Medicine for aching souls? Beauty to counter the ugliness? Answers? We have no answers; we never did.

As I write this introduction a few years later, our hearts have been battered by more bad news: the devastation of hurricanes, tsunamis, earthquakes, and the global implications they all carry on their thunderous backs; a terrible and unjust war, our country's broken promise of rebuilding two countries we attacked, new and unstopped genocide, the bones of our own democracy shaken and rattled till they're loose in the joints, a "war on terror" gone mad. Whoever you are and whenever it is you find yourself reading this book, if the world is still the world, there will surely be new heartaches to add to the litany. As for now and the foreseeable future, here we are in our strange, glorious, struggling, and divided country, walking not toward a "Murky Unknown," but within it. The communal dialogue may have quieted now, with many pretending that all is well and sliding back to business as usual, but others still wonder a very great deal about "probing the depths of the human soul," and about what that means in these times, and about how to do it.

And not one of us has The Answer. Thank God.

An old Hasidic story tells how once—this was back in the Old Country—a young scholar named Moishe studied the holy texts day and night, night and day, with pleasure and love and devotion. Until one day he looks up from his books and says, "Wait. Wait! What is the meaning of life?" He closes his Talmud and goes flying out into the streets, waving his arms and shouting into the air, "What is the meaning of life? Somebody answer me! What is the meaning of life?" People come running from their homes and their shops to see who is carrying on like this. "You won't believe—it's Moishe!" They chase after him and try with all their might to calm him down—to no avail. "I cannot study one more verse of Torah or look at the Talmud again until I know what it is, the meaning of life!" Shlomo suggests he should go see the rabbi three towns away. And that's what he does. He goes.

When at last the old rabbi invites the young man to his study, Moishe's too anxious to sit. "Rebbe," he whispers hoarsely, "tell me, I beg you. I cannot go on eating or dancing or studying or praying until I know how to answer it: What is the meaning of life?" And he gazes at the rabbi with relief in advance, because surely this man of greatness and wisdom will know and will tell him.

The rabbi stares at the student a long time without speaking one single word. Then all of a sudden he hauls off and whops him so hard in the face, Moishe falls to the floor.

"Why did you do that? What have I done? I was only asking, What is the meaning of life?"

"You fool!" says the rabbi. "Wake up! Consider! You have such a radiant question! God forbid you come up with an answer. It's the answers that tear us one from another. It's the questions that hold us together."

Our society is quick with answers. Every ad we see is an answer: "What will make you happier, richer, thinner, more regular, less headachy, more enviable, more sexy, more spiritually enlightened? Our product." Almost any politician who wants a hair of a chance to win doesn't waste time with dicey questions, but throws out two-bit "answers" like tootsie-rolls from a float at a parade. When a NASA Mars probe failed big-time some years ago, it was reported that the scientists had been instructed to collect their answers about the universe in "the cheapest, quickest, and most profitable manner." So they blew it.

Of course there are often and necessarily vibrant, ingenious, hard-won, and critical answers to difficult questions, and thank heaven the honorable search for them seems hardwired into us. But our work in theatre presses us to scratch out deeper and deeper holes in the dirt with our fingernails to get at the roots of the most succulent *questions*, the ones that will hold us together.

This book offers one way to dig those holes, and suggests some good places for digging.

It is *not* the "only way." There *is* no "only way." May we forever be protected from "only ways."

THE LIVES THAT SURROUND US

> The story of one life cannot be told separately from the story of other lives. Who are we? The question is not simple. What we call the self is part of a larger matrix of relationship and society. Had we been born to a different family, in a different time, to a different world, we would not be the same. All the lives that surround us are in us.
>
> —*Susan Griffin*[2]

Not long ago I went to a traveling exhibit on Mongolia at a nearby art museum. Starting with a large, felt *yurt* filled with the exquisitely crafted objects that gave it life in the old days, the exhibit traced Mongolia's history through the time of Genghis Khan, through Soviet control, up to the present. At the entrance a poster asked in very large letters: "Why should Americans care about Mongolia, a country located halfway around the world with a population so small that it would not fill one large U.S. city?" I squinted at that for a minute. The implication of course is that fundamentally, anything Distant or Small should not be of concern to us, we who are Here and Big. An old and lethal habit of ours.

"Why should Americans care?"

"Because," said the poster, "we have something in common." Oh. Not because we are different, which is inherently interesting, challenging, eye-opening, maybe even humbling; not because we might be overcome with awe at another way of life, or gain some insight into the larger story of humanity; not because we might have something to learn from and/or give to the Mongolian people. No, we should care because we have something in common. "Americans and Mongolians," said the poster, "both love our independence and freedom, and had to fight for the right to self-determination and democracy." End of discussion.

But isn't the question "Why should Americans care about . . . [fill in the blank]" obsolete? And isn't it a withered, lungless voice that asks it? Increasingly, the prescient ones among us point to the sorrow and warn of the dangers of our national self-absorption and our systemic ignorance of the rest of the world.

We in theatre, whose crazy joy derives from expressing *self* by entering, embodying, and expressing *other*, must be hearing another voice

---

[2]Griffin, Susan. 1992. *A Chorus of Stones*. New York: Doubleday. p. 168.

rising up around the world now: a Voice-of-many-voices, less arrogant, rigid, and provincial and with far more care to spare—a voice which asks, from its ten-thousand landscapes and in its countless languages, more blood-filled and useful questions about how we are to proceed as humans, and which recognizes the dreadful price we pay for our forgetting that *the story of one (or one culture's) life cannot be told separately from the story of others.*

One wonders what it would be like now if, after the terrorist attacks on our country—when we felt that the world had changed, when our strangely complacent sense of security was shattered, and when we began struggling with collective misery, loss, fear, and confusion—we had as a nation, and as a matter of course, turned with humility and respect to the many peoples around the world and in our homeland who have long dealt with such misery, loss, and confusion? What if even in our grief (or perhaps because of it) we had begun looking *outward* for guidance and help? But instead, we turned more inward than ever, thickening and hardening our borders into impenetrable barriers that we might keep the world out and wall ourselves in, that we might "protect" ourselves from life and the suspected threats it carries, that we might ensure our continuing deafness to the wisdom of hundreds of millions who know all too well about massive pain, massive shock, and massive loss, as if we had nothing to learn from the ways in which others' souls endure.

We who are Here and Big stride out to the rest of the world either to attack it, exploit it, or teach others what we know to "help" them be like us. It has not been our national predisposition to complete the circle or give it more meaning by sitting at the feet of other peoples and asking what *we* might learn from *them*. It is a gift that our theatre could be offering in abundance today, a conscious, graceful, and spirited reach to *connect* the courage, beauty, majesty, or wisdom of one people or culture to that of another somewhere else—strengthening both, however invisibly, in that act.

HEALING: FROM THE OLD ENGLISH "TO MAKE WHOLE"

The practice in the book is subtle work having to do with subtle energies. And Subtlety is not our middle name. Although there's a peculiarly American brand of embracing complexity with a gutsy, innovative,

American brilliance and delicacy, our nation's overarching personality leans heavily toward the big and the bold. It believes things it can touch, weigh, buy, sell, and show as trophies. It likes loud music, over-sized meals, big bank accounts, and giant TV screens. Our mainstream mind these days is blind to and even contemptuous of the subtle, the small, the sacred, the invisible things that hold life together and sing our true spirit.

We may perfect our own version of it, but we Americans by no means invented this style of myopia. In Africa there is a tale about a farmer who loved his cows for their superior milk. One day he notices that they're producing less of it, then less and less, day by day, till one night the farmer hides in his field to see who the thief might be. Glancing upward, he sees a star in the sky growing bigger and brighter, then descending to earth, and then—oh my God—it lands right there in his pasture and turns into a gorgeous lady.

"You're the one who's been stealing my cows' milk?" he asks.

"Correct," she says without even looking ashamed.

He could have had her arrested, but he falls in love instead and asks her to marry him. The star-lady accepts on one condition. "I have with me a basket. If I come to live with you, you must never ever, ever open my basket." No problem.

So they marry and live together and everything is fine.

But one day while his beautiful wife is outside, the farmer's curiosity has its way with him. He sneaks over to the basket, opens it, and peers inside. And then he begins to laugh and laugh and laugh, slapping his sides, wheezing and coughing from the hilarity of it all.

His wife appears at the doorway. "Have you opened my basket?" she says.

"Yes!" he guffaws. "And guess what? There's nothing in there. Nothing at all! There's absolutely, positively nothing inside!"

The star-lady grabs up her basket and storms out of the house.

"Wait!" cries the farmer. "Don't leave! I love you madly!"

But she is already ascending into the sky, calling back as she rises, "What is inside this basket is spirit. How utterly typical of you humans to imagine that spirit is nothing."

And he never saw her again.

Our acting training focuses primarily and wisely on strength and flexibility of body, voice, imagination, emotional accessibility and responsiveness, and intellectual analysis of text. Traditionally, we have left the "basket" untouched and unmentioned in a dim corner of the studio. But although what's inside it is impossible ever to grasp fully and pin down, still it is those invisible, ineffable, uncatchable qualities of soul and spirit we long for in our theatre today: what's "in the basket," after all, is what we refine body, voice, imagination, and emotional channels to express in the first place.

It was mentioned earlier that the practices in this book derive from what's called "spiritual healing." So what on earth is that? Among other things, spiritual healing has to do with flows of subtle energy both within and around us, with shifting states of consciousness, with meeting places of spirit and matter, with the literal force of love, and with the intricate craft of "making whole" that which has been fractured or disintegrated.

There are those who'll start wriggling around and wanting a cigarette, even if they gave it up 20 years ago, or go running off in all directions at the mention of such things. It's understandable; there is a lot of flakiness out there, and much that's ridden in on the New Age caravan is perceived by many as suspect. For some it's suspect because it seems weird and gooey, does not subscribe to a rationality-is-all point of view, and gushes about auras at cocktail parties. For some, it's because it's all become one more glossy, hyped-up mega industry, spawning books and sets of audio tapes that tell you how-to-become-a-millionaire-plus-spiritually-enlightened-in-our-three-week-program or how to lose-forty-pounds-while-opening-your-third-eye-and-without-giving-up-chocolate. Others may be suspicious because so many things are tossed together under the New Age rubric that it can get confusing. There are things within its frame which are indeed shallow, superficial, self-involved, hopelessly humorless, cloud-voiced, and maddeningly blind to the harshest realities of the world out there beyond the meditation center.

But along with the fluff and the woo-woo, there have also come some exceedingly rich and useful teachings, perspectives, and practices from many traditions around the world which are anything but flakey, pastel, shallow, or narcissistic. They are made of fire, thorn, and wind, blood, bone, and soul, and of the hard-won, well-worn sacred experience and wisdom of the ages. We do well to learn from them.

Although they may complement one another, such traditional teachings are not interchangeable and aren't meant to be thrown willy-nilly into the same pot of soup and swallowed mindlessly. They can be, and sometimes are, misunderstood, exploited, ripped off, stripped of context, cheapened, and/or abused to serve our own crunching hunger for something meaningful in a frantic, materialistic, techno-driven culture. On the other hand, much of what has resurfaced and been adapted to our place and time is being taught and taken in with depth, refinement, respect, and reverence; many people are reaching out to learn, remember, and/or reclaim sparks of genius from other ages and other peoples to re-illumine our understanding of who we are, where we have come from, what we are part of, and what we might become—every one of which questions is at the root of worthwhile theatre.

The art of spiritual healing is very old, rooted, and practical. It comes in many forms from various cultures where it has been perceived as life-giving and useful, rather than glitzy or glamorous, and where there is no shame in perceiving our health and well-being as deeply intertwined with the state of our spirit and its relationship to the universal whole and/or the holiness of the universe. As mentioned before, the specific kind of healing I speak of here has primarily to do with the energetic fields surrounding and permeating our physical selves.

While *For Love of the World* itself is not a manual on the art of healing, I have found from years of studying the healing arts and experimenting with its possibilities in the context of theatre that the connections are helpful and significant. In the end, however, healing and theatre are distinctly different arts, and though I celebrate throughout the book their fertile interface and introduce certain aspects of healing work with which I hope you can deepen your art, it is never with the notion that we confuse the two callings. Instead, what is offered here is given in the spirit of continuing the dialogue begun some years ago about how we in theatre might move forward in a way that matters to and serves us at this time, how we might better "probe the depths of our common soul," and how we might be encouraged to keep trekking together through the questions.

Chapters 1 through 3 are reflections about *why* and explanations of *what*. *How* it all applies directly and practically to your writing and performing does not come round till Chapters 4 through 7. Patience.

All of it is written with the hope that we whose strange work by its very nature has no borders will travel far and wide, listen acutely, embrace with tenacious grace, and transmute into magnificent dramas the stories with sparks of holiness hidden inside, not only to bear witness to our human soul's inscrutable puzzle, not only better to comprehend the shimmering world of which we are an inseparable part, but also to learn something of how to walk unbowed and head-on into the winds of the Murky Unknown warmed by the vision and fearlessness of other such pilgrims from every corner of the world who are heading in the same direction.

Scientists tell us that the flapping of a butterfly's wings in Peru affects a snowstorm in northern Siberia. We are the butterfly. And we are the storm.

1

The Song in the Story

The world, the human world, is bound together not by protons and electrons, but by stories. Nothing has meaning in itself: all the objects in the world would be shards of bare, mute blankness, spinning wildly out of orbit, if we didn't bind them together with stories.
—Brian Morton[1]

FIRST STEPS

A journey of a thousand miles, as the saying goes, begins with one step. I used to think the first step was just that: one foot in front of another, and step-by-step you will get to your goal a thousand miles away. A teacher set me straight: "The first step," he said, "is determining your direction. If you travel a thousand miles north when you needed to go south, you're in trouble." Ah. So the first step, then, of one's journey toward dramatic monologue is deciding what *kind* of stories we choose to perform, in what *manner* we wish to tell them, and to what *end*. That's our direction and our compass all at once. The landscapes and terrain will vary wildly within and between each such journey, but we do set out with one essential understanding, that drama is always about one thing: the nature of humanity.

While other art forms have broader possibilities, ours illumines only Us: who we are, how we love, hate, struggle, create, destroy, desire,

---

[1]Morton, Brian. 1998. *Starting out in the Evening*. New York: Berkley. pp. 184–185.

bless, pray, rage, grieve, act through or defy our human spirit, perceive or misperceive each other and the world, affect or are affected by each other and the world, how we live, how we die, how we dance or stumble in between. *The Cherry Orchard* is not about trees and *Cats* is not about felines. As dramas they are fashioned from *our* (not the trees' or the cats') perspective, and from *our* manner of expression. Two roots of drama being human presence and human language, we're forever bound to the telling of our own Story, as we lack the language, and usually the comprehension, to speak for the other living presences on earth upon whom the "who we are" of us actually depends. Each has its own stories—creature, tree, weather, landscape, every kind of thing or force—but they are not communicated in our form of language. So the role of theatre, whether it plays it well or not, is to probe the *human* story. Historians, psychologists, anthropologists, and sociologists do so too, but only we must alchemically transmute the raw materials of our research into a concise and embodied poem from and to the human heart, immediate, and intimate.

Annoyingly obvious as it may sound—"Oh! Drama is about human nature? I never guessed!"—it doesn't always seem to be the common ground our American theatre walks. If we truly believed that a devoted probing into the hidden corners of the human spirit were the crying need we say it is, we might for one thing toss out the notion of *minority theatre* and nurture as a matter of course a theatre concerning humans of every conceivable background, experience, rhythm, culture, environment, history, perspective, color, and song, as the greater the range the more revealing and incisive the view of our common and disparate soul. We'd be crawling on our collective knees across ten thousand diverse landscapes of space and time, knocking at every door for a glimpse of every kind of ourselves, seeking out dramas from and stories of one another, gathering up the most textured visions of our face and timbres of our voice from both home and far away.

"Write what you know," we are instructed. Absolutely. No question. And "know thyself," we are taught, before attempting to know others. Good advice. The problem is how we've gone about it. After a century of psychologizing, we Americans, singly and as a nation, have come to believe that knowing ourselves means turning only *inward* and focusing obsessively on oneself, a practice that could lead to our resembling the mythical Klang Bird who flies around and around in increasingly smaller concentric circles until it finally flies up its own ass.

But all honest writers and actors know in their bones that to know oneself—as individuals, as a society, as a species—one has to know other-than-oneself. It is not possible truly to understand our story if we are ignorant or dismissive of the stories of humans different from ourselves. As many are cautioning us today, Americans cannot viably continue to presume that we can cut ourselves off from the maelstrom of the rest of the world and have the least sense of human reality.

Wishing to write of what we know and yet grant that our own story is part of something broader and more complex, our task in theatre now is to stretch, reach out, and struggle to know more. As the philosopher Gurdjieff said, "If you want to know how you walk, find out how others walk—then you'll know."

There are, of course, fine monologists who themselves come from peoples and experiences considered by the dominant culture to be *other*, and who write of what they know from within the world of the unheard, the dismissed, the disenfranchised, and forgotten. The theatre community as a whole might support more and more of these voices and insights to broaden our collective comprehension of who we are, where we come from, and where we are headed. But here too, within the framework of writing from your roots, each informed and concentrated view needs wide edges interfacing with a larger picture.

I am a Jew. As I write this chapter, Jewish settlers are being forcibly taken from their homes in the Gaza Strip by mandate of the Israeli government. Today there's a front-page photo of a sobbing woman dragged from her home by two Israeli soldiers who themselves are weeping. She's crying, "This is a pogrom!" Her neighbor yells, "A crime against humanity!" It's a side of the story which might cause one's heart to stand still in pain. But the story, as all stories do, wears another face as well: in this case, long ago in the same spot, others were forced from their homes to make way for this one. And while a heart may stall at a one-sided, tunnel-visioned view of human suffering, it shivers and is moved from a more expansive view, from its willingness to embrace the tension and unrest within the complexity of the broader reality.

In 1989 during the first Palestinian uprising, I went to Israel and the West Bank and listened to Jewish and Palestinian women speak of how their long-shared historical conflict informed their personal lives. The resulting solo drama inspired by those stories had at its heart the tension of their two realities colliding, sometimes even in the same voice, creating what Susan Griffin calls "the dangerous tremor in the line between I and Not I." Here are two small stories from that piece—one from an Arab, one from a Jew—two seeds in that trembling ground reflecting how even in one soul, a story's diverse sides are pumped through the same heart.

The first is from Brurya, a 60-year-old Jewish teacher from Jerusalem.

BRURYA

You think we don't know we have a reason to feel fear? You think we don't tremble inside our skins? Look, once I was in Beersheba at a teacher's meeting, ya? And it was late at night, I said, "How will I get home?" They said, "Oh nothing, there is a taxi." So they take me to this taxi and I get in. And the driver talked, so right away I knew he was an Arab—because with us, you know, you cannot always tell who is who just by the looks. So we start to go, and we have to go through all these Arab towns, and I am looking out the window, and there are only Arabs on the streets, and I'm this Jew alone. And then he stops on the road, and he picks up two Arab men, and I am sitting in the front near the driver, and these two Arab men, they sit behind. And I am shaking like this. I'm afraid to look forward, I'm afraid to look back. So after some time, these two men they argue about the price, they leave the car. And then I don't know which is worse, that they are in the taxi or no. Anyhow, we went.

After a while the driver stopped the car. And I was sure that now he will kill me, or maybe he is bringing someone else to kill me, and I was so frightened I stopped breathing. But he was taking benzine—how do you call it, gas—for the car, and he got back in and we went. And it was completely silent. Usually I talk to drivers, you know, but I was like this [shaking]. *I was shaking so hard my head was rattling.*

After what seemed like three years, we get to the Jerusalem taxi station and he turns to me, he looks at me, he says, "You were very frightened." I said, "Yes." He said, "I know it." So I took some money to pay him. He said, "Where do you live?" I looked at him. . . . I told him. He said, "I will take you there— no charge—so you will see, not all Arabs are killers." And I know we were both thinking at that moment, There are those who are! *But he was telling to me, "Not me."*

And I was so ashamed, you know. I was so ashamed. But to go alone across the lands of the Arabs! Look at me! I am not easily frightened! But that night I thought I'd die of fear. And he was so nice. He was so nice.

The second story is from Nouha, a 40-year-old Palestinian teacher from Ramallah. Note here too how the complexity of it all is part of her reality.

NOUHA

I remember the beginning of it here when we people began to open our eyes and start fighting. For me, I remember the day and the hour. I had come home from the school where I teach and was here in my front room. Outside I heard shouting. One young boy had thrown one stone at a military car, and from that my world turned its corner. All the soldiers came crashing into people's homes in the neighborhood. They beat people. They destroyed furniture. They came into my house, and they threw down every chair, they turned upside down every table, they smashed whatever their hands could take. And I sat there and I watched them. I just sat there, holding my little girl, who cried. And I said, "Why do you do this? I did not do anything. Why do you do this?" And I told them what was happening in my mind. I said, "I am sitting here in my home with my daughter, and you come in here out of nowhere and frighten my child and cause many troubles for me. Now I am obliged to fight you. You force me to have a heart against you."

My own sons now are burning tires and throwing stones. We say nothing about this to each other, but silently I am proud of them. Because if they want their independence, they must learn to pay with fire and blood. They must know what struggle means. They must pull themselves up and try to do something by themselves for their people, just as the Israelis have done.

And I drive my little girl through the streets of Ramallah, through its rubble and its sadness, and I point out to her the soldiers and all the marks of the occupation. I want her to know what it means not to be free, so she will know what freedom means when it comes, just as the Israelis know their freedom now. And I say to my daughter, "This is a soldier, but you must understand, not all Israelis beat and kill people. There are those who wish us to be free. And you must know this and learn how to separate." And I take her to meet with the Israeli women who come to this city to work with us. My little girl, she sees it all. But I think she does not yet understand. She is only three. Yesterday someone asked to her, "What do you wish to be when you grow up?" And she said, "I want to get one of those stone slingers and start throwing stones at the Jews."

The power of our theatre now will be in its desire and capacity to bring together the renegade, wrestling, contrasting, disparate threads of stories within stories within stories and to plait them into a thick, thistly, great-hearted fullness that binds us together as we stand without keeling over within the questions they engender.

WHY THE JOURNEY TO BEGIN WITH?

In this Age of Information when we're clobbered day and night with news of the Human Story, we may wonder what's left to know or probe about our soul. An alien from another planet observing our morning and evening rituals of taking in The Tale of Humanity through the media might think we're engaged in a form of prayer, so religious are we about it. And if, to understand us more, said alien were to follow our lead and take in that same daily news of the human story, with some filler from the entertainment industry to wash it down, he'd most likely return to his home planet with a damning report: a story of ceaseless violence, corruption, stupidity, myopia, greed, addiction, power-mongering, hypocrisy, self-absorption, ignorance, cynicism, war, torture, killings, exile, famine, terrorism, pandemic disease, natural disasters, ecological collapse, child soldiers, child killers, corporate rule, lack of imagination, inarticulateness, ugliness, pettiness, shallowness, trivial pursuits, provincialism, cheapness, the consumer index, and instructions, when things get really bad, to keep shopping.

This is the tale of us that we ingest every single day. What do we do with this grotesque saga? Where in our bodies, psyches, or souls do we stuff it in order to function with any faith in our viability as a species, or to believe that whatever we're embarking on each day has hope or meaning? And wherever it's hidden away, what is it doing in there: rotting? infecting? hibernating only to wake up one day and send us into psychotic collapse?

Not that we should numb ourselves from the harsh and painful truths; perhaps we turn away from them too much to remain intact. Lately, in the face of natural disasters, war, and genocide, we're informed that we have "compassion fatigue." But how can that be? Compassion has no limits; it does not tire or wear out from overuse. The fatigue might be instead from the undigested anguish, fear, and anger, with so little in our daily story of substantial, meaningful protein or promise to buoy us up or help us navigate rough waters. This is a different brand of buoying than our hearing on the news—tucked merrily between the bombings, beheadings, and ecological disasters—of a happy resurgence in the sale of hula hoops.

One of the most pressing tasks and possibilities of our craft is to make the bitter, sharp-edged parts of the human story literally palatable and digestible. And at the same time, to keep alive and visible, with as much grace, saltiness, and integrity as possible, the larger weave within which the strands of the world's pain are threaded. If we present the ugliness, however honestly and intelligently, with only cold, slick cynicism, it's not enough. Though it's always a relief to hear sane people lament articulately of the horrors and stupidities, when that's all there is, it usually just fuels our anger and despair. For while the misery in the story is not false, it is not the whole or only truth of us, and swallowed on its own in consistent overdose levels it is, quite literally, toxic. So here we are, a people so terrorized and depressed by the human story that we move through the days with a gun in one hand and Prozac in the other, armed and sedated. On the other hand, if we shut out the painful truths and settle for sugar-syrup drama, we're out of our minds.

Peter Brook has written that theatre has the power to speak to the unmet needs of its time and place, and to answer a society's hunger for what is lacking. What needs within us now are unmet? What is lacking? With tales of doom and destruction crashing like tidal waves at our heads and hearts, what kind of story might inspire a theatre that could feed the hunger of our own time? What do we wish to be seeded at the thumping heart of our work which might sprout into actual nourishment?

There is a Pygmy tale in which a little boy goes wandering through the woods and hears the most beautiful song in the world. He searches through the trees and in the undergrowth till he finds the small bird singing so grandly and, cupping it gently in his hands, he runs back to his village.

"Father, Father! We must give this bird some food!"

His father, sweating hard from one chore and another, tosses a pinch of millet toward the child, and commands him to take the bird back to wherever he found it and get to work. The boy does as he is told.

The next day in the forest once more, the little boy is enthralled to hear it again, the most beautiful song in the world. He listens, he dances to the music, he finds that bird and carries it carefully home again.

"Father, Father! Here is the bird who sings the most beautiful song! We must feed it!"

The father grinds his teeth, throws some grain toward the bird, and gives his son the same instructions as yesterday. The boy does as he is told.

On the third day when the child trots home again with the song-bird and calls out for it to be fed, his dad blows a gasket.

"You have work to do! Leave that bird with me, go back to the forest, and come home this time with some firewood." The boy does as he is told.

As soon as the child is out of sight, the father picks up his axe, swings it down once, and kills the bird. When he kills the bird, he kills the most beautiful song, and when he kills that song, the man himself drops down dead, just slides to the ground without a sound, all the breath in him gone.

I told this story to a friend who said, "God, how revolting and depressing. Is there no redemption?"

There is.

First, there is not and never has been only *one* most beautiful song in the world, or even one *kind* of such song, or even one singer. If that seems paradoxical, that's exactly the edge our theatre has to dance. Second, he who had no time to hear and feed the song may die figuratively or literally, but the "little boy" in all his hundred million shapes and incarnations will always be wandering out in the woods of the world listening for that music, dancing to its melody, and finding its singer, wise with the understanding of what needs to be fed.

There is a hunger now for stories singing that song of beauty at the root of us, connecting us to our own souls and to all of life. There are holy sparks in such "music," the heat of which can crack us open heart and soul. We speak of theatre that moves us, touches us, or rubs us the wrong way; but these days being moved, touched, or rubbed in any direction is not enough. We need more of those ecstatic moments when theatre *cracks us open* like seeds, that we may take in through the crack more of the grief for our world and more of its beauty. Both. Together. At the same moment. Not in a line, not in tidy segments with commercials in between, not to manipulate an idealized balance of good things and bad, but both sides of our reality smashing against each other like waves crashing from opposite directions and becoming one wave. It is the ability to hold it all at once that is itself the germ of true story born of life's ironies. And in the embrace of this tension, no matter what the topic of our drama, arise compassion and humor, two regal paths of perceiving and moving through the world, without which—what's the point?

LOOKING FOR WATERS OF LIFE

In studying human anatomy you learn that for physical movement to occur there must be an oppositional force working against what wants to move—that is, for one muscle to stretch upward, another, however subtly, must move down. And so it is with hearts. For a heart to be moved enough to be cracked open, it needs to be touched by *an opposition of forces*. It's not a matter of Pollyanna goes to Bosnia, a gloss of sweet to counter the nasty or some cockeyed attempt to tack onto the bad news a cheery little addendum as a fuzzy upper. It's that the bones of our human story are *made* of opposition, and their marrow is irony. It's what we are. It's how we sing. It's the ocean in which we swim.

Maybe it's the very breaking of our hearts that spurs us in the first place to gather and mend the pieces of the broken vision of who we are on this earth, which is another irony: that a brokenness should help us with wholeness.

We hear in Russian folktales of the magical "Waters of Death and of Life." In "The Firebird," the young hero is killed and hacked to pieces by his evil brothers. First a vial of the Water of Death is poured over the severed, jumbled pieces of his body, and they come together as a whole. Then when the Water of Life is applied to the lifeless form, it fills the boy with warmth and breath again; he jumps up, alive and older. We might imagine such a theatre, devoted to seeing clearly the dying and disjunction *and* to carrying life-giving waters, a theatre that in its stumbling and assuredly incomplete ways had the heart and the ambition to re-member the dismembered fragments of our collective understanding and infuse us with new breath, that we might become a little older, maybe even wiser. It is possible. It does happen in those inexplicable moments of theatre that cleanse and renew us for that moment in time, as if washing us with the Water of Life.

So we choose the heart-cracking tales of life which hold the human cruelties and losses, yes, but which also uncover within the ashes the sparks of intricacy, eccentricity, defiance, resilience, laughter, reverence, generosity, daring, brilliance, mystery, wildness, grace, delicacy, and fiber, the strength to grieve mightily and the grace to bless magnificently. For these qualities are also of our common soul, yet they are stunningly and systematically absent from our daily information diet that features mostly madness and pain on its menu. It's like being in one of those super grocery stores half a mile long with forty aisles and ten thousand shiny packages of what looks like food and sells as food, inside which warehouse, if you look long and hard enough, you might find one-quarter of one side of one aisle labeled "Nutrition." Our work is that small section of that one aisle in a morass of pretend food.

We hunger as well these days for sanity. The word (from the Latin *sanitas*: health) reeks unfortunately of *sanitized*, and heaven knows it's not a sterile, latex-gloved lucidity we crave, but the wild, untamed sanity that drips with mud, ash, sharp teeth, and storm, a sanity which shimmers with wonder, wit, guts, and the flame of spirit. To create drama deliberately about sane characters is not what you'll be advised to do in playwriting programs, and heaven help you if your press releases announce "A hot, riveting, not-to-be-missed show about sane people!" If blabbing out loud about a Theatre of the Sane will not be your ticket to success, it may be because we've come to confuse sanity for the predictable, the rational, the sensible, the boring, the normal, the bureaucratic, the objective, and the suburban. It isn't.

The normal is not necessarily sane. Consider the little madnesses all around us, and begin to note how they affect you even though we're so accustomed to them we barely notice. Tiny daily things. Commercials. Not only the insult to the brain many of them are, but note the context into which they intrude, then note the minute responses in your thoughts, emotions, body, spirit. A TV movie about global nuclear war arrives at the dropping of the first hydrogen bomb and cuts to a commercial for Fruit of the Loom underpants in which grown men are dancing around in giant fruit outfits—a banana, an orange, a bunch of grapes—singing a ditty. A TV special on the life and death of Judy Garland, emphasizing that diet pills led to the addiction to the drugs that killed her, is sponsored by a company selling diet pills. You bring home five small items from the drug store, spend half an hour hacking and slicing away at the needless packaging, and fill garbage cans with their unrecyclable bulk when we know we can't afford the waste.

Those are one-one-billionth of one thimbleful of the little ones. Try to observe the sensations within you, however subtle, each time one comes your way. Then note your responses, in all parts of your being, to the bigger madnesses, as when our own government, the veil freshly lifted by hurricane winds from our neglect of poverty-stricken citizens, concocts a budget-saving bill that takes billions from those very citizens while continuing to offer gilded, lucre-laden baskets to the rich. Or when we see wars begun and countless lives shattered for reasons having nothing to do with reality. The madnesses are legion. Many of our responses actually occur in our invisible force fields, but more on those later. For now, when you think of it, just observe when, where, and in what manner you feel them. This kind of ongoing, unframed practice is what is called an *arpeggio* throughout the book—a small exercise you can do when the spirit moves.

Then observe the effects on any part of your being at a moment of sanity. If, for example, a miracle happens and you hear the *truth* told by someone in power with forthrightness, integrity, personal responsibility, or an admittance of life's true complexity. Or when you experience an unexpected act of decency, sacrifice, or deep intelligence; or when you come upon something fashioned of beauty, hard-won skill, and love of the doing, without tackiness or slick packaging to cover shoddiness at the core. What actually and literally happens in mind, heart, and body at such times? Later, after reading Chapters 2 and 3, it might be helpful to come back to these arpeggios and consider how your subtle energies are responding to the sanities and insanities that surround us.

Unlike madness, which can be boxed, labeled, and divided into neat categories to better understand its manifestations, sanity cannot be so circumscribed or neatly defined; its complexities, possibilities, and diversity defy categories. Like snowflakes, no two sanities are alike, and their unique designs are intricate, elegant, and enchanting in their detail. Like the capacity for love living within it, sanity comes in every color that was ever sung into being; and it's worth noting when you see them for real on a stage or in a film, that love, inner strength, strange and startling moves of kindness—often awkward, usually small and weird, never perfect, and always saturated with a kind of fierce integrity—are in fact more compelling to watch and more delicious to ingest than the usual tedium of pettiness, hatred, and violence.

SETTING YOUR COURSE

So you set out on this journey to look for the stories that sing. How to set your course? You listen to the questions that fire you from the core, the ones you've made love to all your life. Disguised though they may be as a theme, an idea, a political issue, the situation of a place or its people, a historical period, a story or set of stories, a compelling character, in the end they're always questions about who we humans are and the nature of our soul. There are ten million different versions of that question. Yours must be your own: honest, homegrown, and from your own heart and soul. If not, no matter what you do to gussy it up as drama, something inside it will be dead on arrival.

There are pulls, passions, and private nagging voices that draw us where we go and shape us all our lives. Some of them nudge their way into our consciousness early on, before we know what to do with them. When I was a ten-year-old kid in suburbia, a neighbor told me stories one night of her years in Auschwitz. I had never heard of Auschwitz. I couldn't even pronounce it. But when she was done, I thought the world I'd known had split in two, and questions crawled out of that chasm and have been emerging from it ever since. There are those times, not many, when each of us is shaken by such moments: a story, a book, an experience blasts through to something at our core, and our sense of the world trembles, cracks open, reshapes itself, and we never see things the same again. Often at those times the hairs of our nerves stand on end, and something starts pulling or pushing us to explore questions and places we didn't know existed. I came to understand later that it isn't the *world* that splits in two at such moments; it's *we* who smash open, enough to let a little more of the world's reality enter, dragging its mysteries with it. For each of us, the focus and the color of the questions will be different; we are, blessedly, drawn to bear witness to different people, different places, different things.

So you follow what truly concerns you, no matter how outrageous your quest appears to others, and you resist going for faddish or politically correct topics that make you look noble and get you a grant. Timely issues themselves are by no means off-kilter; it's the reason for choosing a topic that matters: Are you pursuing it for ego, image, and advancement? Or does your topic, even a hot item in the news, happen to be a variation on the theme of those puzzles you've been nagged by, drawn to, fascinated with all your life? Or possibly something which now, sincerely, has suddenly blasted you open? Those are the ones to go after. And no matter what shape they take in your heart and mind, they must have a reach beyond the small parameters of one's own life and concerns. "How come my friends can eat ice cream sundaes and stay thin, and I gain ten pounds by looking at an ad for chocolate?" is not the kind of question I'm talking about even if you've made love to it all your life. (There's a solution to that one, by the way. My sister's doctor told her—get new ancestors.) It's wide-armed, greathearted questions that lead to the stories that, though specific to time, character, and place, will breathe on us all.

My own pull has been to stories of those far away in the midst of or recovering from deep cultural conflict. So I've traveled to such places, met and interviewed many people for the gathering of stories, and for other monologues have researched in books the poet Carolyn Forché calls "the events of social and historical extremity" of our times. The monologue examples I use here are from that ongoing journey; but it's only *my* journey, not yours, and no better or worse than any other. Depending on the questions that guide you, the song in the story and the crack in the heart may come from watching that homeless man down the block—never interviewing him, just observing over time. You may find the stories you need in your grandmother's kitchen, a battered women's shelter, an AIDS clinic, a PTO meeting. You may be drawn to seek them in Cambodia or the Bronx, the farm down the road, or places that two months ago you couldn't pronounce. You may be drawn to investigate countries where live those we are informed are our enemies. Your inspiration may come from one paragraph or image in a book that sets you searching far and wide. You may be drawn to a historical period and create (from historical figures or your imagination) characters of shining presence within it. One line may open up a world for you. Nadezhda Mandelstam, wife of one of Russia's greatest poets executed for his poems during Stalin's reign of fear, said, "People could be killed for poetry here because we still knew how to *live* by poetry." That one thought could send you to her autobiography, the history of those times, the writings of others who endured them and survived to tell the story, and finally toward a monologue peopled by some of those remarkable presences who knew how to come through hell and make inspired beauty by describing it in a way that empowers us all.

There are those in our own time whose stories cry to be heard in a Theatre of the Sane: the first African woman to receive the Nobel Peace prize, Wangari Maathai of Kenya who instigated the Green Belt Movement and whose work to save her country's environment is a model for us all; or another Nobel Peace Laureate, Aung San Suu Kyi, still under house arrest as she struggles unflaggingly for democracy in Myanmar (Burma); and of course, those unhonored and unknown souls whose work nonetheless keeps the world spinning. The tales (real or imagined) of your own ancestors may call you: the lands, times, customs, and lives they had to leave behind but that still echo in your marrow. So many lives to write about; so many voices worth hearing; so many stories to fire us and bind us together; so few theatrical occasions in our land now that bring them to life.

Poet Mary Oliver writes of "aspiring to a better, richer, self, . . . where I might ascend a little—where a gloss of spirit would mirror itself in worldly action. I don't mean just mild goodness. I mean feistiness too, the fires of human energy stoked; I mean a gladness vivacious enough to disarrange the sorrows of the world into something better."[2]

The fires of human energy stoked, not by fear, anxiety, or tribal rage as is currently the fashion, but of all things, by vivacious gladness. And not a mild goodness as in a yen to be nice (defined in the Oxford English Dictionary as "foolish, stupid, and senseless"), but a gladness so fierce and exuberant it's a bulwark against being flattened by the world's anguish, tempering its heaviness to create something else, something regenerative. Others say it in different ways. Visionary activist Caroline Casey presses us to learn how to metabolize the poisons of the world so that out of that compost comes new life. In the Buddhist form of meditation known as *tonglen*, you learn to breathe in the hot, smoky miseries of life's pain and breathe out cool, clear elegance of beauty in one form or another. Teacher, artist, writer Martín Prechtel teaches that all beauty and all song are born out of our griefs and our failures.

So we set our course to find the stories that bind us, those which sing of our capacity to hold together both the sweet and the bitter. For inside this meeting of forces, we change. They are not the stories in *People Magazine* or on the evening news about acts of honest decency or courage in the face of disaster, splendid though they are to know. They are not the personal memoirs that celebrate one's victimhood and delight in despising the oppressors. Nor are they autobiographical stories of suffering and survival offering no evidence of transformation, no hint of what brings us out to a world where we are not the center. They're a more fibrous weave than any of those things, pushing up from a dense humus of the beauty *and* the grief *and* the failures *and* the

---

[2]Oliver, Mary. 2004. *Long Life: Essays and Other Writings*. Cambridge: Da Capo Press. pp. 90–91.

rage *and* the forgiveness *and* the consciousness of one's connection through it all to a wider world—the shadow of self-pity nowhere in sight.

An arabesque of such stories, spiraling tendrils of human experience arcing around the globe, might possibly bind us together in a life-sustaining way. There are said to be hidden currents of energetic force beneath the earth that connect the inherent power of her sacred sites. They are known as *ley lines*. It is possible to envision a theatre consciously fostering what might be thought of as *human ley lines*: currents of energetic force which harness the soaring spirit of one people or culture to another somewhere else and unite us at the core. It is a theatre for those who crave a place where we can embrace and be embraced by *both* our joy and anguish, and in that embrace give birth to possibility. At such moments there somehow arises a kind of collective courage. "Courage" from the French *coeur*, or *heart*. "Love," writes Galway Kinnell in a poem, "is very much like courage / perhaps it *is* courage."[3] Perhaps it is.

Only if our monologues are made of courageous heart will they be containers strong enough to carry the tangled complexities and coarse-grained ironies of our larger story and to speak from its many-faced, many-tongued body. It may be that in our time we cannot afford anymore to trade our souls and integrity for the sake of ticket sales— pumping out more work fresh off the factory line: the formulaic, two-dimensional, nutritionless dramas wrapped with a plastic shroud of soullessness and choked off from real life. For in settling for the shallow, the slick, or the soulless, we are forgetting to feed the bird. It's an enormous forgetting, a systematic and societal forgetting. And while the result may not be as literal or dramatic as the father's death in the Pygmy story, by not feeding that which sings the truest and most beautiful songs of our humanity, we starve as well, leading us to do things that cause life around us to wither. The very essence of our work as dramatic writers and performers, the responsibility and the luxury of what we can offer, is to feed the bird—by searching for it, recognizing its song, listening deeply, and learning to sing with grace and force for those who come hopefully and hungrily to the theatre, its hundred million melodies.

00:00[3]Kinell, Galway. 1982. *Selected Poems*. Boston: Houghton Mifflin, from "Flying Home." p. 148.

2

Invisible Force Fields

WHATEVER CAN'T BE MEASURED

Until just a few years ago, there was a dangerous section of the Austrian autobahn where there occurred an average of six serious car crashes a year. The Austrian Motorway Authority put up speed signs, renewed the road surface, fixed the bends in the road, but nothing worked; the accidents kept piling up. Finally, in desperation, they conducted a two-year experiment kept secret from the public. They hired Druids to see if they could help. (Yes, Druids, those beings of an ancient Celtic priesthood about whom one reads in Welsh and Irish legends. I was surprised to find how alive and well they are today.) After analyzing the situation, the Druids advised that one-ton pillars of quartz be erected on the highway's roadsides. When the pillars were erected, the number of accidents fell to zero and stayed there.

Later, the Arch Druid explained that they'd "located dangerous elements that had disrupted the energy flow [of the area]. The worst was a river which human interference had forced to flow against its natural direction." The huge pillars, working a bit like acupuncture for the earth, restored the energy lines to their original healthy flow. "I admit," said an engineer from the Motorway Authority, "when we first looked at it [the energy lines], we were doubtful. We didn't want people to know, in case they laughed at us. But it was really an amazing turnaround."[1]

---

[1] *The Sydney Morning Herald* quoting the *London Herald*. August 11, 2003.

Meanwhile, as we're laughing our heads off anyway because there's something hilariously wonderful about the whole thing, Austrian scientists have dug in their heels even in the face of the facts. "Whatever can't be measured," proclaimed one, "does not exist. These energy lines and their flow cannot be grasped or measured, and their existence is therefore rejected by scientists."[2]

This chapter is not a discussion of Druids, about whom I know little, but of those energy flows which can't be measured and must therefore not exist. It is an entrance into the ways those seemingly esoteric currents relate quite practically and usefully to our work in theatre. First the explanation, later the specific connections.

Everything has an invisible force field of undulating energies we might not *see* in the usual way, but to which we are always responding and always interacting. This force field informs all that we are and do, and we're actually more aware of it than we realize. Force fields are as familiar, ubiquitous, invisible, and immeasurable as love or hate or jealousy or altruism. Like the one by the autobahn, every river has its own invisible force field. Every storm, landscape, tree, mountain, rock, and plant; every kind of creature whether it flies, swims, crawls, leaps, howls, buzzes, snorts, or sings has its own energetic field. And so, of course, do we—even those of us convinced that no such thing exists because it can't be weighed or measured.

These fields of subtle energies surround and permeate our physical bodies, and in their frequencies our material and spiritual selves are bridged. While our own culture on the whole has traditionally dismissed such things with a snort and a sneer, many peoples of this and other eras have lived comfortably with a down-to-earth understanding of their complex reality. For those of us in theatre, an ability to comprehend and perceive the workings of these subtle energy fields, within which our individual stories throb and take shape, and through which we are connected to the overarching field of energies around us (the Larger Story), grants us deeper, more ornate and more expansive relationships with text, character, and audience. It can spice and thicken, as with a fine French sauce, specific qualities of writing and performance. When we develop a fictional character or base one on a real person, knowing how to sense the qualities of that imagined or actual being's

---

[2]Ibid.

energy field, and understanding how to adjust our own energy patterns according to specific elements of its design, can lead to entering more fully and resonantly that unique personality. It's a way of singing the woven strains of that story's melody and of touching, however subtly, the fine and invisible threads of spirit running through it.

The truth of the matter, which had better be acknowledged, is that in your finest, most honest and soaring moments of performance, you're doing it anyway, intuitively. Part of what this book is about is what's happening in those radiant moments and how to move toward them more consciously and consistently. And hopefully you'll come to a point one day where the conscious steps to getting there become unnecessary—the terms and deliberate preparation having become second nature. For now, more explanation.

Our own invisible force fields go by several interchangeable names: *the human energy field*, *the subtle body*, *the light body*, and perhaps the oldest of these, *the aura*, a term that's dangerous to toss around too glibly because it causes some people to lean in too close, all limp-eyed and gooey-voiced, and others, like that Austrian scientist, to go screaming into the hills. But as mentioned before, there are many (including scientists) who have been comfortably and pragmatically familiar with these things for a long time.

You could say that these invisible force fields are made of a kind of music—music that arises from waves of energy streaming in manifold patterns of vibration, density, direction, frequency. Somewhere, in a range far beyond our capacity to hear it, we hum. Everything is vibration humming at different frequencies. Some peoples say that the world began with sound, that everything is born of sound's vibration. The Hindus say that the seed sound of all life is *om*. The Tzutujil Mayans live and pray with the understanding that all that manifests in this world is spoken or sung into being by the speech of the gods. The Aborigines follow the song lines with which the spirit ancestors sang the world into being. The Bible says, "In the beginning was the word." What we see as solid matter, including ourselves, is pulsing, vibrating waves, a complex and infinite layering of song we don't catch with our ears, but one we swing to nonetheless, and that we continually shape and are shaped by.

So here we are—we and everything else on earth, made of atoms dancing to their own music. We know, though our minds reel with the wonder of it, that if you were to blow up an atom to the size of a football field, the nucleus in the center would be the size of a tomato seed, and the electrons spinning at the outer edges the size of salt grains. All else is a huge ballroom of space, the appearance of solidity coming from the singing, swinging motion within it. In a way we waltz, fox-trot, clump, limp, boogey, or sashay around to the rhythms of our own force fields, each one a part of the larger field surrounding and holding us all in a cosmic symphony of interactive movement and relationship.

Normally—though who can define normal—the subtle body of a human being extends about three feet from the physical body in all directions: up, down, side to side, front and back. Some perceive it as egg-shaped, others like a giant spherical bubble. There are times when it expands and grows very bright, as when you're on stage performing at your very best, connected to a force beyond yourself that's true and beautiful. At other times it can contract or grow dull, as when you're in pain, or do something incredibly stupid and everyone's seen it, or for that matter, when you're giving a manipulative and dishonest performance.

Each person's subtle body is comprised of distinct and interpenetrating levels of energy, all expanding outward from the physical body and each level a higher frequency than the last. Though different traditions speak of different numbers of these energetic layers, for our purposes (in Chapter 3) I'll focus on seven. In one sense, the material body might be seen as the field's densest and most slowly vibrating level, slow enough to be perceived by our everyday senses, and in this respect, I'll sometimes refer to the whole (the physical and subtle bodies together) as *the body-field*.

While distinct and individuated, every person's subtle body is an integral part of the universal field of energies holding and transmitting the life-force that keeps us going. It is through the boundaries and certain energetic centers of our personal fields that we take in and digest that life-force for which English has no single, unhyphenated word, but other languages, of cultures for whom its essence is more commonly accepted, do. In Sanskrit, for example, this life-force is called *prana*, in Chinese, *ch'i*, in Japanese *q'i*, terms becoming more familiar to us these days. This *prana* is the breath of life, "the force that through the green fuse drives the flower," the spirit of vitality within and around us, the blood-flow of the greater mystery sparking, feeding, quickening, and connecting our individuated and inscrutable selves to one another. In return, we inform the larger field with whatever pulse or music is coming from the configuration of our own subtle energies as they reflect our thoughts, feelings, actions, and state of consciousness. The condition of our personal fields—what affects them from the outside world and how we ourselves inform them knowingly or unknowingly—is what allows or prevents this exchange of *prana*.

Although the human force field has its own anatomy and physiology, within that common framework we each have, as with our physical selves, a unique arrangement of subtle energies that is, was, and always will be recognizably ours, its energetic constructs and emphases peculiar to our own story, experience, heredity, thoughts, dreams, environment, predispositions, and personality. There is no perfect subtle body to aspire to, any more than there is a perfect physical body to despair over not having (no matter what Madison Avenue spends trillions of dollars hollering). Our energetic fields, responding always to what is within and without, are in constant flux, usually in delicate moment-to-moment shifts and realignments, but sometimes they change in more profound ways, either over time or from sudden major events. What occurs within our energy fields informs directly every aspect of our being.

Following are some exercises to begin sensing the subtle energies, but first a word about centering and grounding, the key to all the exercises to come.

CENTER AND GROUND

The traditional home base of acting training is learning to center and ground, which is the same exact foundation for those trained in the healing arts where centering and grounding are essential for a full and conscious perception of the subtle energies. In both disciplines, the center is described as a few finger-widths below the navel in the middle of the lower abdomen. It is there that we send our breath, from there that we extend our *roots* into the earth. This belly center is understood to be the primary storage place for our energies, our personal gas tank of sorts. It's here that our energies are gathered, warmed, enlivened, and held until necessary; and from here that they flow when we need them. To center is to *collect* the disparate energies which have a tendency to fly off in all directions, and to *anchor, warm*, and *strengthen* them in the breathing belly. To ground is to *connect* from that center to the pulse of the earth, quite literally to tap into the earth's heartbeat, whose frequency is by its very nature stabilizing, vitalizing, healing. The point in centering and grounding is not to stuff and leave one's energies inside the belly or down in the ground. On the contrary, it is to provide a clearly delineated and stable container from which coherent energies can fountain up and travel into, through, and out from your whole body-field.

Center and ground, therefore, are not rigid states, but ride on the breath in delicate, constant motion. So as you proceed through all exercises in the book, remember to check that you're breathing deeply into your center. When focusing intently, we often tend to forget to breathe at all.

Exercise: Centering and Grounding

You can begin in one of two positions. Either sit comfortably, soles of the feet on the floor, with a relaxed but straight back and closed eyes; or stand with feet hip width apart and pointing slightly outward, knees bent and loose, pelvis relaxed, spine comfortably straight. Take a few slow, full breaths.

For the next seven breaths, breathe into your whole being a clear white or golden light, and exhale any tensions or obstructions from body and field, visualizing their exiting from all over your skin as dust, small flecks of debris, maybe a soft brown mist. After those initial seven breaths, let the warm, clear light which enters you on the inbreath fill your belly center, and imagine that center glowing with warmth and a calm strength. On each outbreath, imagine the warm light condensing into a small, shimmering, iridescent ball. Continue with this for six more breaths, in and out, feeling the expansion and the contraction of the light and the warmth with each cycle, but not a diminution of these energies.

Now root down into the earth from that quickened belly center. Try doing so in each of the three following ways; then as you continue this practice choose the one that works best for you. In all cases, send the root straight down from your center.

1. Visualize sending a light beam or a laser line down into the hot pulsing core of the earth and matching some of that heat and vibration in your belly.
2. Send the light beam from your center not to the core but to the dark, moist earth around it filled with underground springs, roots, and rock.

3. Imagine you are a three-pronged plug, and one light beam goes straight down into the earth from your center, while two others travel from the belly across to your hips, down each leg, and through the soles of your feet straight into the earth, so there are three main roots plugging into the earth's energies.

You might visualize a root system growing from the central roots and spreading horizontally through the earth below you, holding you firmly on and in the ground.

It is your focused attention combined with the power of your imagination that turns on the juice of what actually happens.

Keep breathing and be patient. When you sense a rooting, the important thing is to take in through those roots the pulse of the earth's energy and to allow it to flow upward through your feet, then through your whole being. Make sure too that it flows into your heart and from there down your arms and into your hands. You need not strain to pull this energy up as if hoisting a heavy bucket from a well; if the connection is true, earth energy will bubble up of its own accord.

Though it may take a while at first to make clear connections with this rooting, over time you will come to do it in a matter of seconds. Knowing how to center and ground in an instant is especially important for performing monologue where there is no one else on stage to restabilize you when you feel wobbly or uprooted. It is also the main gateway into perceiving the subtle energy flows, and so this practice is the first step of all the exercises which follow.

There is a second step aligned with center and ground which you will not find in an actor's usual training.

INTENTION

In the healing arts, setting a clear intention is, with center and ground, the foundation from which any meaningful restoration occurs. Arriving at a clear intention and developing the dedication to follow it is not synonymous with wishful thinking combined with ego or raw will, but rather a pull from within your soul and then your conscious mind in a direction that is true to who you are at the core, beneficently aligned with a greater will than your own, and life sustaining both within and beyond the situation at hand.

Intention comes in many sizes, from immediate and small ("I will eat this grapefruit slowly"), to broad intentions encompassing a lifetime's endeavors. ("I choose to make of my work something of hard-earned beauty and of service to this world.") There's setting your intention not to yell at Phyllis even though she got the part you wanted and you know she mugs her way idiotically through every role. There's setting your intention to take more risks at this evening's rehearsal because last night you were lazy, or to sense subtle energies in a given exercise in whatever form they come, or to be an honest actor and not a superficial one, or to learn everything about birds or how to play the mandolin really well, or setting your intention to do what it takes to make your body stronger. For healers working with a client, the built-in assumption is that part of the intention is that whatever transpires be for the highest good of that client—which may well be something your own intellect, diagnosis, assumptions, or best-laid plans cannot foresee or even sometimes understand. It's a good idea for us all.

There are various ways to come into a clarity and fullness of intention; some require moving to a dimension of being and consciousness even deeper than that of the subtle body's pulses.[3] For our purposes, however, a simplified process is in order—especially with monologue, for as with center and ground, you will encounter those times in a performance when you will quickly and blazingly need to re-ignite that intentional flame.

Exercise: Intention

- Center and ground.
- Consider your heart, for now, to be the seat of your intelligence. Let the earth energy rise through your feet, through your body, to your heart, warming it in your mind's eye with a silver clarity. Set your intention there, whatever it may be, feeling the heart fire up as if the flame's gone on in an oven. Your intention can be articulated in image or words or both.
- Consider your mind, for now, to be informed by heart. Let the silver light rise to and fill your mind with the same warm, silver clarity and the same lucidity of intention. Imagine your heart, your

---

[3]See, for example, Barbara Brennan's *Light Emerging*, pp. 287–304: a chapter on "Our Intentionality and the Hara Dimension," a thorough and excellent map into the territory.

mind, and gradually your chest in between, to be warmed and charged by the silver flame of your intention. This is not a soft, hazy light; it's more like the sun glancing off crystal.

- Mirror the same strong charge in your feet and hands, your pelvis and throat, then throughout all of your body, always keeping it grounded in the earth. Set your right hand on your heart and your left on your belly with the intention of keeping the light of that flame balanced and coherent.

After some practice, this simple exercise (without the hands on heart and belly) can be done quickly and invisibly offstage or on, even in the middle of a performance.

EXERCISES TO SENSE THE SUBTLE BODY

1. On Your Own (standing or sitting)

- Center, ground, and set your intention to perceive what you can.
- Rub your hands together vigorously for a few moments till they're warm and tingly. Then shake them out. Hold your palms facing each other about eight inches apart, relaxed and slightly curved. Move your palms toward one another and back again, a slow, gentle pulsing in and out. They should not touch. When they come toward one another—a few inches apart—it's like you're touching the edges of an invisible ball. Keep the hands relaxed, keep the movement in and out, slow and easy. See if you gradually begin to feel something between your hands—a warmth, a tingling, a density of one sort or another, a magnetic pull of the hands toward or away from one another. If, after a few moments, you still feel nothing, shake out your hands, rub them together briskly again until warmed, gently shake them out and try again. It helps to have your eyes unfocused or closed.

Different people may feel different sensations, but whatever you feel between your hands is your own energetic field.

2. With a Partner

- Stand facing each other, a couple of feet apart. Breathe, center and ground. Choose who will do the energy sensing first: this is Partner A. Partner B stands still, arms relaxed at sides.

- Partner A: Rub your hands hard till they're warmed, then shake them out. With palms relaxed and gently curved, place your hands a few inches away from the outside of your partner's arms, and slowly, gently pulse them in and out from the body of your partner. Relax your eye focus; your perceptive energy here is in your hands, not your eyes. Keep moving your palms gently in and out toward the outer arms of your partner, never touching the physical body. Gradually see if you can pick up a sensation—again it might be warmth, tingling, a magnetic attraction or repelling, or another quality of *something* there. You might feel it through one hand and not the other. You might feel something at the top of the arms and not lower down. This doesn't mean there are breaks in your partner's energy field, just that there are certain places you're able to feel what's there, and certain places you cannot yet perceive it.
- Note what you've felt, and now Partner B gives it a try.

3. *On Your Own*

- Seated, the soles of your feet on the floor, eyes closed, breathe, center, ground, and set your intention to focus and sense what's there.
- Imagine a bubble of energy surrounding you, starting at the crown of your head, just an inch or two out from your skin. Move in your mind's eye slowly from your head down to the soles of your feet, body part by body part, seeing what you can sense of this bubble. Don't force a sensation into your imagination, particularly one of angelic perfection, some diaphanous cloud of sweetness and light. Just connect with whatever qualities you can honestly pick up, charming or not. You may be able to feel it only around certain parts of your body. It may feel clogged and thick or delicate and incandescent; you may sense it as a color, temperature, or texture in certain places. Be careful not to judge, interpret, or try to *fix* or change what you feel. Who knows what the story is? Just notice it with open curiosity and attention.

The human energy field is not synonymous with human spirit but is a sparked network of crossroads where our material and spiritual selves meet, and understanding it can strengthen our capacity to enter and express theatrically the myriad permutations of the human mystery. Within our body-field (that is, our physical and subtle bodies together), spirit is forever spiraling into matter, and matter into spirit, the workings of these invisible force fields grandly and exquisitely mysterious. They are by no means occult forces for a chosen psychic few to comprehend; in fact, we all perceive them day by day, moment to moment, in a profusion of ways we take for granted.

Consider, for example, how you feel when you've fallen madly in love: expanded, strong, electric, glowing. When humiliated or belittled, on the other hand, you can feel shrunken and small, a dry and brittle nutshell. Depression turns us gluey and heavily weighted. In anxiety or fear we fly off, jittery, in all directions. When confident, we can feel a coherent vitality. We speak at times of feeling "beside ourselves," "out of our body," "jumping out of our skin," or as if "the lights are on but nobody's home." These descriptions are not merely figures of speech but reflect directly what is happening within our subtle energies as they expand or contract, cohere or scatter, sit easily with our physical bodies or jump away from them in one direction or another. It's important to note that our thoughts and emotions are themselves waves of energetic vibration, creating strong nuances within a field, informed by that field in turn, and strongly affecting the energies of those around us.

Sometimes we meet someone about whom we know nothing and think, "Oh *that's* someone I really want to get to know," or conversely, "*There's* someone I don't want to touch with a ten-foot pole." What is this intuition? Part of it is the pulsing rhythms of two separate energy fields beating against each other in harmony, dissonance, or something in between.

Some people can see these fields in color, form, and light; others can feel their texture, density, temperature; some *hear* their vibrations, and some just intuitively know what's going on. We've accorded a kind of glamour to being able to see the fields, but it doesn't mean much. There are other ways to sense them, and all of us feel certain qualities of the subtle body's movement and condition to one degree or another in ourselves and others. We know when we or other people are ungrounded, uncentered, weighed down, lit up or dulled, a giver or a thief of energy, sharp edged or cloudlike—all of which states mirror the condition of the force fields.

ARPEGGIO: LISTENING TO YOUR FIELD

As you move through your days, notice the shifting, changing qualities of your subtle energies according to how you feel, what is happening to you, what you are thinking, doing, or desiring. See if you can name the qualities. To a great degree, you will sense the energetic goings-on in your physical body and emotional state. Note when you feel sluggish, ill at ease, anxious and ungrounded, centered and full, jagged or tight, fluid and calm, connected or cut-off. You do not need to meddle with it unless you want to; simply pay attention.

FORCE FIELDS OF PLACE AND COMMUNITY

Groups, communities, and societies of human beings also develop fields of common energy, sometimes very quickly, sometimes over days, months, years, or centuries of shared culture, experience, landscape, language, and history.

There are events which can very suddenly catalyze the shape and nature of a group's force field. The thrill of one's home team winning the away game creates ripples of electric energy rising from a common core of the group on one side of the stands. A beautiful wedding or moving funeral can bind the guests, strangers to one another just two hours ago, in a common field. Many of us remember how when President Kennedy was assassinated, most of our country was welded together in a common field of stunned and grieving energy. On September 11, 2001, it happened again in a different way, the force field of our whole nation bruised and shaken. Teachers know that every class of students comes in with and develops its own personality or energetic field, and no two are ever exactly alike.

Every theatre ensemble develops its own unique force field during the period of rehearsing a show, as do performers and a given audience for just that one night.

Natural and human-made environments have their own energy fields whose energies reflect their histories past and present. I was in Bosnia not long after the war there, teaching in a decrepit hotel which had a sickening feel about it, as did the river at its edge. Each day as my two American colleagues and I walked over the river's bridge and into the hotel, we would feel vaguely dizzy and disoriented. Later we learned that during the war, the hotel had been used as a rape center where women had been incarcerated and repeatedly abused, some of them killed on the rooftop, their bodies thrown into the river below. The ugliness still alive inside the history of that particular place was not an abstraction, but an actual energetic presence in the building and the river; there were huge, unhealed wounds imprinted in the force fields of that place seeping into our own fields.

Even in the weeks of our daily gatherings in the hotel with women displaced by the war, something in that atmosphere began to shift. It was not by any means a cure or remedy for all that had been lost and suffered, but a tiny noticeable realignment of energies from the accumulated hours and days of new energies these women brought into the space with their fierce spirits, their dignity, their having a place to come together to tell their stories, to weep, eat, sing. The simple acts of their daily endurance began to sew together in some few small places the rips in the energetic flow of that whole place. As the energy shifted, people began to relate to themselves and one another in different ways, and every act of generosity, tenacity, or kindness was itself a small mending of broken energies. A year later when I returned, the feel of the river was startlingly clear (the natural world may have greater healing capacities than we humans). The hotel was getting better but had a long way to go, and who knows how many generations that might take. This subtle mending of the story's field is not the same as literally rebuilding the structures and thoroughfares of a disaster zone, in which rebuilding may or may not heal its field at all; sometimes it covers over with a shiny gauze the still-festering wounds beneath, unseen but still felt.

Bosnia is an extreme example, but our subtle fields are adapting to the vibrations of environments all the time in daily ways. You may walk into a room where there's just been an hour of bitter argument and pick up, as we say, the vibes. You may be in a fragile wispy mood and feel the sudden uplift or tonic of being with someone filled with high and shining spirits. When you come into New York City, you usually have to adjust to its jazzy, busy buzz, and it may take a day or two after leaving to unwind. At the seashore, on the other hand, your subtle body—and through it your physical body, mind, heart, and spirit— calms, opens, and relaxes (except for some New Yorkers who could get antsy from all the quiet).

Simply *imagining* yourself in one place or another, as in the exercise below, can cause your subtle energies to shift in response to the field of that environment.

Exercise: A Sense of Place

- Center and ground. Set your intention to keep your energies and senses open to what you imagine.

- Visualize yourself in a series of contrasting environments, conjuring in your mind's eye as many specific sensory details of these places as possible. As you imagine each environment, note your subtle energetic responses.
- You're in a crowded, fluorescent-lit shopping mall the week before Christmas. Visualize the sights, smells, pulse of the people there, the tastes, textures, temperatures, rhythm, sounds, and note what they do to your energies. Do they make you light up? Close down? Become tight or relaxed? In or out of your body? Do they speed up your own rhythm or slow it down? Etc.
- Breathe out those images and sensations, and imagine yourself now in a sun-baked piazza of an Italian hill town entering a large old stone cathedral. Feel the cool, dark belly of the church, high ceilinged and quiet but for the echoes of footsteps on the stone floors. Smell it. Feel it on your skin. Again note any changes in sensation in your body and/or subtle energies.

You can try it with such places as a circus, a dense forest in early spring, Fifth Avenue and 42nd Street at rush hour, an ocean beach, a sleigh ride in a freezing blizzard.

Be as specific as possible about where and in what manner you feel your responses: in physical body, breath, thought, emotion, or sense of presence.

I know, I know, it is not big news that we feel differently in different places or situations, which is precisely the point. We don't tend to consider the cause of what we already sense: that the vibration of our own music changes in accordance with the rhythms we enter or that enter us vibrationally, shifting the tone and the shape of our force fields and informing the state of our being.

CHANGING THE RHYTHM

These energies are called subtle because their frequencies of vibration are higher than that of matter and are therefore more subtle to detect compared to the concrete, sensate, weighable obviousness of our physical selves. When, many times each day, we consciously or unconsciously shift the predominant qualities of our subtle bodies according to need and circumstance, it's usually without considering *what* in us is being so reorganized.

Performers do it all the time, both on stage and off. In character portrayals we strive mightily to walk a different walk, sing a different
tune, exude a different color than our own. Sponges that we are, we
tend to practice it offstage as well, copying someone's gait along the
street to see how it makes us perceive the rest of the world when in that
body, imitating the timbre, accent, or patterns of someone's speech for
an inner whiff of that story, pretending—because we can't help that
mad delight in trying on *otherness*—to be in someone else's skin. In
playing around like this, we're altering the structure and workings of
more than body, behavior, and tone; we're momentarily rearranging
some of the design, texture, and rhythm of the energy flows that make
our body, behavior, and tone what they are. As we do so, rewriting our
music and altering even our state of consciousness, the subtle energies
of who and what are around us are shifted as well in an unending communication of vibration.

There are times when it works like harmonic resonance or musical
entrainment when, as with a tuning fork, a musical tone causes the
vibration near it to match that same frequency. You might be flying off
in all directions, but find yourself calming and coming down to earth
when with someone whose field exudes those qualities. You might be
with a friend who's sluggish and depressed and find yourself sliding
down that same slimy hole. Not that we are energetic clones of one
another. A depressed person might just as easily cause you to turn rab-
idly irritable. An anxious, ungrounded group of people could drive
your subtle energies into similar uprootedness, or cause you to counter
the anxiety with calm and integration. Whatever the response, it is
energy bouncing off, conjoining with, informing other energy; it's consciousness in dialogue with consciousness.

Exercise: Energy Emphases

This exercise is inspired by a far briefer one in Robert Benedetti's *The
Actor at Work*.[4] I used Benedetti's exercise in acting classes for many
years before I knew of the human energy field, but once I saw how the
exercise could connect to subtle energetic structures and sensations, I
shifted its focus to allow for a sense of the way our fields inform our

---

[4]Benedetti, Robert. 1976. *The Actor at Work*. New Jersey: Prentice-Hall, Inc.
pp. 83–86.

bodies, emotions, perspectives, and relationships. What resulted can be done on your own or in a group. It's a long exercise now, but worth the ride.

- Center and ground.
- Start walking through the room in whatever way comes naturally to you at the moment. We'll call it *neutral*. Be aware not so much of what your subtle body is doing as simply that you *have* one and that it fills and extends beyond your physical self. You will be asked to create emphases of energy flow at different areas of your body-field, exploring the polarities of upward or downward flow, front and back, in and out, etc. The energy shift happens through your imagination and intention.
- Keep walking, and now imagine that ninety-nine percent of the energy in your field is radiating to and from the *front* of your field from head to toe. Keep moving. Sit down, stand up, change your direction, but keep moving. Notice what this emphasis of energy in the *front* of your body-field does to

  your breath,

  your pace,

  your rhythm, both inner and outer,

  your emotions within this energy emphasis, and

  your perspective on the people and things around you.

Stay with it for a couple of minutes.

- Breathe it out, and walk in neutral for a few moments.
- Now through your imagination, shift the energy emphasis to your *back*. Ninety-nine percent of your energy is running up, down, from, and toward the *back* of your body and just beyond it. Give yourself time to make the shift and really feel it. As you move with it, sense your responses with this new energy to all the things above.
- Breathe it out; walk again in neutral.
- Shift the energy emphasis so that ninety-nine percent of it moves *upward*, flowing up from your waist, through your chest, through your arms and hands, up through your neck, and out the top of your head. Move around with this strong *upward* energy for a few moments, and explore the same responses as before.

- Go back to neutral for a moment or two. Breathe deeply.
- While still walking, shift the energy emphasis to a *downward* strength—all the energy pouring through your pelvis, down through your genitals, down your legs through the bottoms of your feet. As you move, attend to the effects this emphasis has on your walk, emotions, perspective, etc., as above.
- Go to neutral, breathe deeply, walk around.
- Move your energy emphasis to *outside* your whole body, letting it radiate outward from the edge of your skin, almost no energy inside the body. Explore the same responses, taking your time. Breathe it out.
- Walk in neutral.
- Move the energy *inside* your body, in a tiny pea-sized point inside your chest or belly. What are the effects of this energetic shift? Breathe it out.
- Walk in neutral.
- Imagine that your energies are now *broken* and *stuck* at certain places: neck, waist, joints. It therefore flows *erratically*. Explore the specific effects for a few moments. Breathe it out.
- Walk in neutral.
- Shift your energies to move *freely* and *smoothly*, both inside and outside your body, *fluid* and *coherent*. Note your responses in body, emotion, breath, and point of view. Breathe out.
- Walk in neutral.
- Last set of polarities: Imagine all the energy in your field (and therefore body) as profoundly *weak*, *leaking* out at the joints and through thin boundaries. How does this inform your movement, feelings, breath, etc? Take your time. Then breathe it out.
- Walk in neutral.
- And finally, all your energy in physical and subtle bodies is *strong* and *powerful*, filled to the brim but not overflowing. Stay with it. How does it make you breathe, affect your pace and rhythm, your feelings and your perspective of self and the world around you? Breathe it all out, and ground again.

If you have done the exercise on your own, jot down your responses to each set of polarities to clarify and remember them. If with a group, come together to compare the most pronounced sensations and effects you felt with each set. You will probably find differences. For example, with a strong *back* energetic emphasis, one person might have felt strong and powerful; someone else paranoid, another pulled backward against his will. With a *down* energy, some may feel grounded, others depressed or stuck. What has happened is that the nature of each energetic shift of emphasis has combined with the current configuration and flow of your own subtle energies, leaving a particular imprint and response which may differ from that of someone else whose subtle energies began the exercise in a different state.

If all is vibration, if we and all else are not solid, atomized entities but actually waves of motion, then we are all, as we hear from many sources, quite literally connected—without suits of armor or plastic shields to cut us off from one another or the rest of life. Buddhist monk Thich Nhat Hanh calls it *interbeing* with all creation. But this is not a oneness predicated on sameness; rather, it thrives by virtue of *difference*. As Thomas Berry discusses in his books about the story of the universe and our human place within it, life itself and "human formation is governed by three principles: *differentiation, subjectivity, and communion*." Of our world today he notes that

> our present state is a violation of each of these three principles in their most primordial expression. Whereas the basic direction of the evolutionary process is toward constant differentiation within a functional order of things, our modern world is directed toward monocultures. This is the inherent direction of the entire industrial age. Industry requires a standardization, an invariant process of multiplication with no enrichment of meaning.[5]

We in theatre, seeking the stories that will bind us together and striving to express the soul's song in those stories in ways that nourish and animate, might do well to lace our work with a palpable sense of these humming force fields, at once fantastically differentiated and yet, by their nature, interwoven in enduring communication and interplay.

ARPEGGIOS: NOTICING

Part One

- Notice people. Listen to them. Feel the material and invisible forces of their presence.

---

[5]Berry, Thomas. 1999. *The Great Work*. New York: Bell Tower. pp. 162–163.

- Pay attention to how they make you feel. Opened? Closed? Strengthened? Diminished? Charged? Nervous? Frightened? Hopeful? Loving? Calm? Smart? Stupid? Irritated? Bored?
- "No blame," as the I Ching says. Our own energy fields play an enormous role in our reactions and responses to others. If you are bored by someone else, it does not always mean he is inherently boring. Someone might cheer and energize one person and make another feel stupid and belittled. One person is inspired by a teacher, another unmoved. These are the interweaves of energies: unique complex story confronting and relating to unique complex story. Beware of "Oh, her hard and condescending energy field! I am being belittled. Poor me!" Get over it. Just notice. Go at it with what some meditation teachers call "a kind curiosity," as if you're listening for how two strains of music might be harmonious and rhythmically amenable, dissonant and expressive of contrasting beats, or working together as they negotiate how to fit, interact, or arrange themselves for some manner of relational expression.

Part Two

- Keep noticing people. (Never stop noticing people.) Listen to them. Feel the material and invisible forces of their presence. Observe especially people you don't know well, where there are no prefabricated assumptions to muddy the view.
- Pay attention to how you perceive their presence in *themselves*. Do you feel this is someone who is *in her body* or out of it? Charismatic? Timid? Directed? Fractured? Defended? Vulnerable?
- You may sense the qualities of a person's energies as texture, temperature, sound, image, or color. Be as specific as you can in both sensing and describing what you perceive.

Part Three

- Notice the rest of the world. (Never stop noticing the rest of the world.) Whatever our human story is, has been, or will become individually or collectively, it exists within and because of all the presences and forces around us. Try though we have for centuries, we cannot rip our own story from the context of all the earth and think we understand anything. Remembering that all things have their own force fields affecting all other fields near and far, pay attention to them wherever and whenever you can, discovering what qualities of pulsing energy they carry.

One of the differences between our own work with subtle energies and that of healers is that we in theatre are not attempting to heal those whom we observe, portray, or perform for. The people who inspire our dramatic characters and the characters themselves, both real and imagined, possess individual force fields which will *not* be neatly and tidily organized into some nirvanic alignment. On the contrary, because we trade in life's most gnarly vicissitudes and complexities, and because drama at its heart grows from tension and conflict, we encounter and create subtle bodies far from textbook models of "this is how a field should be when all is working perfectly." We are not looking for "perfectly" and we won't find it anyway. Our role as writers and actors is *never* to set out to mend or overhaul the rhythm and configuration of such energies, but to learn to perceive and articulate with as much integrity and respect as we can the *story* that such force fields hold.

We do aim for communion; we do strive for those magical moments when an evening of theatre rises to a place of being a healing or even a holy force, and if it does, then hallelujah, what a glorious gift. But we need to set our intention to create a *container* for such a moment without calculating or manipulating results, the magic arising more from forces bigger than we are than from our best-laid plans. There is indeed something lovely and fine when with all fierce humility one approaches one's work—as a short-order cook, a tour guide, a nanny, a teacher, an artist, an anything—as a medicine path, moving consciously or unconsciously into being a one-of-a-kind medicine man or woman in meeting the pains and struggles of life. It's an honest and beneficent pull and lacks the controlling edge that comes with predetermining a specific curative result of one's performance. And even if a healing container is created of an evening of theatre, it does not make us literal healers any more than theatre's occasionally being therapeutic makes us therapists. Heaven help us if we write or perform from the airless altitude of "My spark-filled work is going to heal this audience and through it the world by Thursday." At best, it's simply inappropriate. At worst, the flaming arrogance is an insult to any audience and a sure killer of the ineffable human spirit which sometimes does bring performer and witness into profound communion.

By *spirit* I do not mean religion, mind you, which would be a certain Alcatraz to our endeavors. But given that our mandate is the exploration of human nature, we must admit it consists of more than mind, body, voice, and emotion, and that all of the above are lit by that enigmatic aspect of our humanity most difficult to articulate or analyze. Though we will forever fail to trap or categorize what we are so hungry to understand, still we must try over and over from a hundred million angles to touch and express its scent, echo, and glimmer of holiness. And in those magical moments of theatre when it happens and we feel ourselves collectively blessed with its breath, for all its immeasurableness, we know it. And it helps us to remember and to re-member who we are.

Our work then is not as healers or therapists, and despite writings in the last decades that have argued otherwise, it seems neither helpful nor accurate to think of ourselves as priests or shamans. We have our own exquisitely medicinal ways of entering and embodying the diverse strains of our human story and of illuminating the spirit that sings of life and binds us together. As we gather in what we can of each story's complex reality, as we dance to the configurations of a character's music, as we shape and offer out that music as one small, prayerful clue toward comprehending the unsolvable mystery of us in relation to ourselves and to this world, we work our own humble brand of shape-shifting. And, without our labeling ourselves anything other than what we are, it is meaningful and magnificent enough.

3

The Subtle Body's Basic Anatomy

BEWARE OF THIS CHAPTER!

This is a dense chapter packed to the gills with information and practice concerning the design and workings of your energy field. While some of you may wade straight through the whole thing with interest and ease, others could start feeling bogged down or kidnapped from your desire to comprehend how these "out-there" concepts and terms actually apply to your writing and performing.

So a word of advice: You do *not* have to plow through the whole chapter to get to the other side. Think of it as a warehouse to hold the theory and basic skills you'll be using as suggested in subsequent chapters, or in ways you concoct yourselves. I encourage you to read through Part I of the chapter for an overview of how the subtle body is constructed, then do what you want with Part II where the exercises are shelved. You might try one exercise after each section of Part I, or skim through without practicing them yet, or skip them altogether for now and come back to them later when needed. As these exercises are most effective when done repeatedly over time, there's really no rush to take them on in one fell swoop this minute.

Okay, you stand warned. If you start feeling a bit overwhelmed by (or sick of) it all, find the nearest exit and *move on!* You'll be needing to come back to it later anyway.

PART I
Subtle Anatomy 101

An explanation of any intricate and cryptic system has its advantages and disadvantages. It helps to illumine the structure and deepen our understanding of something mysterious, but it can also make the miraculous appear more simplistic a reality than it is. To study the anatomy and physiology of the human body won't help us grasp the full miracle of its workings; a knowledge of music theory will not explain the wondrous effect of music on our souls. So too with an outlining of our subtle body's anatomy: it's just a finger pointing to the moon, not the moon. What follows is a basic introduction to an infinitely ornate patterning of light, color, music, and motion, a little like a child's introduction to the orchestra. A professional healer must know far more detail of the energies' workings than we for whom a handle on the fundamentals is enough to inform and enrich our own craft.

In this chapter, you'll be introduced to four elements of energetic anatomy:

- the seven major levels of the field,
- the major energy centers, or *chakras,*
- subtle boundaries, and
- character emphases of will, reason, and emotion.

For far more detailed explanations of the nature and construct of energy fields, I refer you to the bibliography, but especially to Barbara Brennan's *Hands of Light* and *Light Emerging*, on which this chapter's discussion of anatomy is heavily based and to which I am indebted.[1] It was the four years I spent studying with Brennan that initially inspired my transposing some of the tenets of healing arts into the realm of theatre. What you'll find in this chapter reflects that particular thread of healing study.

Compared to the considerable intricacies of physical anatomy, there's a refreshing simplicity to the subtle body's composition, but learning it leads to an appreciation of how the infinite variations of its aspects working together lead to endless diversity. For writers and performers, it's that very uniqueness and complexity we're after, not stereotypes or

---

[1]Brennan, Barbara Ann. 1987. *Hands of Light: A Guide to Healing Through the Human Energy Field.* New York: Bantam; Ibid. 1993. *Light Emerging: The Journey of Personal Healing.* New York: Bantam.

stock representations of good old predictable humanity. Every human energy field is, to one degree or another, a mix of strength and weakness, articulation and murkiness, openness and defense, shimmer and dullness. It's how it's meant to be. We come into this life with some of our personality already sticking out from the folds of our baby fat. (Hang out with infants when you can and watch the mini-character traits, infant opinions, and signs of the unique souls they're expressing even before they're one year old.) And then through our lives, our fields both reflect and influence the unfolding of our personal stories. Through our thoughts, feelings, actions, and experiences, the condition of our subtle bodies can be enlivened and/or damaged in endless ways both small or large. The energetic effects of these events combines with what we came in with, what surrounds us, and our story up till then.

Individuals who experience love, beauty, stability, and respect in childhood will not necessarily turn out perfectly stable and decent people, but the marks of that goodness usually live in some fashion in their energetic construct. Those who endure some manner of harm, whether physical, psychological, or emotional, will carry that battering in the energetic body in the same way as physical injury leaves wounds and bruises on the material body. Many of our energetic wounds, of whatever depth or kind, can be mended or realigned over time, but some may never go away or be healed entirely, their configuration in the field becoming part of the permanent story. Sometimes the energetic effects of suffering will be interwoven with the light, design, or grace already inherent in a given individual's energetic field, or the wounding will be reshaped into energetic form by that individual's mode of survival, expressed in the field as arabesques of light *and* shadow, heaviness *and* lightness, jaggedness *and* fluidity, scream *and* song. It is inside the seed of these oh-so-human paradoxes and counterpoints that our deepest work in theatre lies, and in what is born from their gloriously impossible marriage of elegance and chaos. When we can sense and move into the contrasts living together in the flows of energy, when we grasp those places where brokenness makes love to wholeness, and despair beds down with faith, when we stretch our capacity to hold—as our energetic fields do every day of our lives— the colliding faces of our story all at once, we edge closer to touching our human mystery and singing our human soul.

The two character sketches below illustrate this wedding of contrary forces within our stories, the paradoxes provoking their distinctive, unexpected unfolding. I've chosen exceptionally extreme situations to underline the interweave of light and shadow that operates in all of us, though usually for much less drastic reasons.

1. *Reaching Out, Holding In*

In Cambodia, I traveled with a Cambodian-American man who had been a child in that country at the time of Pol Pot. Shunted from one forced labor camp to another, he saw people die in droves from starvation, overwork, and brutal executions. Even as a child he was a fine flute player, and though the Khmer Rouge had killed the rest of his family, they kept him alive to play their revolutionary songs. His stories of the misery in these camps are harrowing enough, but one of the worst things he carries even now (and "carry" is not a metaphor here; it's a heaviness in his field) is that to save his own life, he was forced to help in the execution of others. It's a memory he may never articulate head-on for as long as he lives.

He is a grown man now. His body is healthy. He laughs, works hard, and enjoys the delights of being alive. But those experiences remain as a black hole in his chest, a gap filled with an invisible weight he cannot ease. Though it is nothing you could literally see, hear, feel, taste, smell, or touch, you sense its presence there—an open gash at the heart of his subtle body. I don't believe he would *want* it to be healed; it may not be helpful or appropriate that it ever leave him entirely.

When the Khmer Rouge collapsed, he escaped and made his way through the jungle to a Thai refugee camp where he was adopted by an American who raised him in the United States. As an adult, he returned to Cambodia to help rebuild its shattered spine and now devotes his life to overseeing some extraordinary projects there. One of the organizations he has founded searches for the few surviving masters of traditional Khmer music and dance, paying them to teach their arts to young Cambodians. It is an exquisite project, and as the old masters blossom from having found some meaning to their lives for the first time in decades, the young ones blossom from drinking in the old art forms, finding new value to their own lives and heritage. The phrase "art can heal" has become a crusty old cliché, but in Cambodia I witnessed its reality, as if small fractured bones of this crushed land were being re-stitched by the care of old and young come together in the name of beauty. Loved and revered by many, my Cambodian-American friend has become a "little father" to many, giving of himself in every way he can to heal, comfort, and inspire the lives of his people.

In fact, his giving is almost compulsive. He can't stop. In Cambodia he is forever tending to this group's needs and that individual's struggle. In America he is tirelessly fundraising for his ongoing work. Loved though he is, he retains an impenetrable shell around him; few are allowed to get truly close or too intimate. It is said by those few left who knew him as a child that even before the years of Pol Pot's horrors, he was special, a greathearted, charismatic being. Now that same charisma and greatheartedness are inextricably bound with the charred hole burnt out of him from unhealable wounds, and what results is an energy design of magnetic and magnificent contradiction.

One might say, "Well of course, obviously, if someone suffers as he did, you are going to end up with an armor about you. What do you expect?" That isn't the point. The point is the extraordinary mix of both outreach and inholding in this one being, and how hideousness and true beauty have joined in a once-only way to reflect the spirit of his story.

2. A *Reed in the* Wind

In Bosnia I came to know and admire a woman who had been a pastry chef before the war. She was an enormous woman—tree-trunk legs, thick torso, massive bosom and behind. She always spoke out forcefully in groups—never rudely or out of turn, but to break an awkward silence or to lift the groups' spirits with her ear-splitting voice, crashing through others' fears or hesitations with her brazen humor and directness. She was a leader, a laugher, a hard-nosed speaker of the hard-core truth. This woman had experienced god-awful atrocities during the war, including the loss of two sons. I wondered then if her psyche had survived the pain in part because she'd been granted a grounded weightiness of body, voice, and field, keeping her rooted rather than scattering in all directions.

One day I used her as an example in a healing lesson for a point about the body-field, something about that largeness and the tough energetic boundaries which seemed to keep her spirit intact. And all the women in the group split their sides laughing. My earthy friend laughed hardest and loudest of all.

"Before the war," she gasped when she could get her breath, "I was a tiny, thin little thing, a stringy reed blown about by the wind. And oh I was so shy. People had to ask me twice to repeat what I'd said because I was always looking at the floor and barely whispering my words. You would not know me," she guffawed, "if the me I was before the war walked into this room right now!" And everyone laughed again so hard, we had to break for coffee.

It is a never-ending miracle what our humanness will do to survive. In the midst of such catastrophe, her delicate and retreating self had fleshed out energetically until her body and her voice followed suit to hold her down onto the earth and move her through the chaos and the pain. Her wound was *in* and *of* that loud and brazen music which had saved and was continuing to save her. Only her eyes, occasionally misting over with lostness and sorrow, reflected the delicate reed she had once been—that slender, whispering self still hiding inside her story and living in her toughened field.

As you read through the outline of subtle anatomy below, consider which aspects of the field's structure might have been informed by the experiences of these two people and in what way; and think of which qualities were strong or resilient to begin with, and which had to reconfigure themselves one way or another. Consider always the strange marriages of a story's dissonant elements that live in our invisible fields.

And on a lighter note, the strains of paradox within us are not, thank God, always about a mix of utter horror with massive resilience or strength. We carry the tangles of incongruent energies in countless daily, less extreme, but often just as compelling ways, as in a Peanuts cartoon I've had on my wall for 30 years:

Charlie Brown is sitting in a chair watching TV. Sally comes up behind him and yells, "I HATE EVERYTHING! I HATE THE WHOLE WORLD!"

Charlie Brown, without turning around, mutters, "I thought you had inner peace."

Sally says, "I do. But I still have outer obnoxiousness."

And there we are.

THE SEVEN SUBTLE LEVELS[2]

The subtle body is comprised of levels of energetic patternings, each with its own qualities and frequencies. Every succeeding level is

[2]Ibid. In this chapter, descriptions of the seven levels of the field, the energy centers (chakras), and the three leanings derive directly from Barbara Brennan's *Hands of Light,* pp. 41–59, and *Light Emerging,* pp. 19–29.

larger than the last, expanding farther out from the physical body like layers of an onion, but unlike the onion each interpenetrates the preceding levels rather than starting at their outer edge. The higher and larger the level, the higher and more subtle its vibrational frequency.

Each of the seven levels corresponds to, informs, and feeds a different aspect of our personality, and all of them influence each other in a web of offering and exchange. This multileveled field of pulsing energies integrates both the earthed and spiritual aspects of us, joining them most forcefully at the heart.

For our theatrical purposes, I'll describe them very simply in terms of their structure and their correlation to our personalities.

Level 1 is a fine mesh of light blue light lines in a pulsing grid hugging the physical body about one-half to one inch from the skin. It surrounds all internal systems as well. This level corresponds to our physical health and well-being, and our sense of being grounded on the earth and at home in our bodies.

Level 2 expands an inch or two farther out, and is a fluid, amorphous level of cloudlike energies, the colors of the rainbow—a bright, clear spectrum when in good health, muted or murky when one's feelings are in disarray. Level 2 holds the flow of our emotions, our ability to feel them with fullness and integrity, and to let them go when necessary.

Level 3, like the first level, is highly structured, a fine net of shining light yellow beams extending a few inches farther out from the physical body. Its pulse, as is true of each successive level, is faster than that of those before. This level has to do with our mental clarity and intellect: our rational, analytical mind,

Level 4, like level 2, stretching out about a foot from the body, is another unstructured level of rainbow-colored clouds of energy, but here each color is mixed with a deep rose hue. This level of the heart is at the center of the span of seven and is a bridge between the lower three levels of the material, earthly plane, and the top three levels connected more to a spiritual expansiveness. Level 4 corresponds to the heart and holds our capacity to feel compassion and to give and receive love.

Level 5, another structured, pulsing net of light lines, extends one and one-half or two feet beyond the skin. Brennan describes it as being negative space within a cobalt-blue field. My own experience of this pulsing grid is of a firm, glistening, silver-white network of light lines. This level has to do with the alignment of our own personal will with a greater force of universal will.

Level 6 has fluid waves of energy extending two and one-half feet from the body. The rainbow hues of this level are all filtered with mother-of-pearl for a soft incandescent glow of color. There is a gentle fullness at this level. On its own it is not particularly grounded, but wide reaching, embracing, generous, and compassionate. Level 6 corresponds to unconditional love, a love more expansive and all-encompassing than the more personal one of Level 4.

Level 7, the last, is once more a finely woven net of light lines, this time golden, extending at least three feet from the physical body. It hums to the integration of all aspects of your being as well as to the connection between your personality and the larger universal heartbeat. It connects body to spirit, and individual field to the universal energies out of which they come, conjoining the uniqueness of who we are in this life to the overarching web of life, past, present, and future.

These are descriptions of the levels as they are in good health. When something is awry—physically, emotionally, mentally, spiritually—the form and flow of the energies reflect that disjunction. Some of the levels might be ripped or torn, leaking energy, stuck and clogged; or the colors might be muted or darkened—in sum, the vibration is not up to par. As mentioned before, no one has The Perfect Energy Field. Our very humanity implies that ultimate overall perfection is not, alas, in the cards. It's the unique permutations that grant us a story in the first place!

To experience the levels of the field, see Exercise 1 in Part II.

SUBTLE BOUNDARIES

Mystics have long maintained and subatomic physicists concur that all is change and flux, and that we are not the isolate, free-floating little mechanisms we've been educated to believe, but are all inextricably interconnected with one another and with all else in the world. When you consider the nature of our living within (and being) vibrational force fields, the notion becomes more magnetic. If we are essentially vibration, our material selves being the densest and slowest vibration of the sequence, then we do not end at the skin with impenetrable barriers embracing us. On the contrary, our boundaries of subtle vibration are not sealed or solid. There's no abutment of brick walls in the meeting of fields, but a delicate meshing and interplay.

In one sense our energetic boundaries resemble those of our cells. For a cell to be truly healthy, it must possess a strong but penetrable border: each cell boundary must be discreet and well-defined in order for the cell to be a coherent, functioning entity; but it must also be *porous* for nourishment to be taken in, assimilated, transformed, and/or released as waste or transmuted energy. If the boundary is feeble or ill-defined, the cell will not function well or will die off. If it is nonporous, its steely closure will also destroy the cell's life.

So too with the boundaries of our auric fields. They must be well-defined to be healthy, so we know who we are as individual personalities and don't merge with the fields of others, losing our sense of self. But to the same degree, the boundary's permeability is essential for authentic vitality and breath. Because *prana* refers to "the subtle energy that propels the universe, the vitality that pervades creation and holds things together,"[3] it needs the freedom to move into, through, and out of our systems. We may well go on living with a hard, tough-nut shell, but within us something will have choked off for lack of nourishment. If, on the other hand, our boundaries are weak or overly porous, we will not know emotionally or energetically where we leave off and another person begins, and we will soak up emotions, psychological states, or energetic forces that do not belong to us, unclear of our own and others' parameters.

For character portrayal we learn to *match* the qualities of another's field, but we don't want to *merge* with them. Actors' own boundaries, while needing to be open and permeable, must also be distinctly delineated as their own.

There are many variations on the theme of mistaking barriers for boundaries, a barrier inhibiting the exchange and fluidity of life-force, a boundary making it possible. As noted in the introduction, changes occurred in our country's invisible force field after September 2001. We developed a new energy pattern called Homeland Security and created fortress-like barriers at our borders in place of a penetrable boundary, to keep fearful things out and our fears locked up within, with windows in the stone walls just big enough for aiming and shooting our

[3]Ueshiba, Morihei; Stevens, John (trans.). 1992. *The Art of Peace*. Boston: Shambala Press.

arrows. The entire country has not by any means succumbed to the fortress mentality, but on the whole this deliberate petrifaction of boundaries does inestimable harm both within and outside of our borders, the permeability of which might serve us better.

But back to mystics, subatomic physicists, and the currents they swim in. That as humans we too are currents eddying within a larger current, that we are not atomized entities bouncing alone through the universe, but conjoined, co-engaged, interlocked, hung together, an inextricable part of the staggering diversity giving life and strength to the whole, speaks directly to our work in theatre. Our investigation and illumination of specific views of the vast panorama of human possibility is nudged in a new direction by this perspective. The individual stories of specific characters directly and literally feed and broaden our understanding of the Larger Human Story. My story, in one sense, is your story, albeit a side of it you yourself do not have to live out in order to grow or change. The story of this raving madwoman, that Mother Theresa, this orphan, or that brilliant violinist who succeeded against all odds is a thread of my story, although they are giving me the gift of enacting that particular piece of the whole. Every unique and unrepeatable melody or story is part of the whole symphony out of which our own melody is born.

See Exercise 2 in Part II for sensing your boundaries.

ENERGY CENTERS: THE CHAKRAS

There are gateways within the subtle body—highly charged points of power where lines of force intersect—that receive, assimilate, and discharge energies from around and within us. These energy centers are called *chakras*, which in Sanskrit means simply "wheel," and indeed they are like little spinning wheels, whirling vortices which pull in the *prana*, the life-force, around them to be metabolized, sent through the system, and, where necessary, transformed.

There are hundreds of chakras throughout the subtle body, like constellations of glowing stars in the night sky. Of these, however, there are seven brightest stars in one large constellation running in a line up the body-field from coccyx to crown. These are the seven major chakras that healers work with for clearing, balancing, and strengthening the field.

Each of these energetic gateways corresponds to, feeds, and informs specific qualities of our selves, behavior, and personalities.

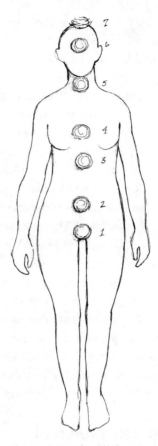

Figure 3-1. The chakras

Understanding their nature and their functioning, and learning how to keep them open, charged, and running well can serve us by keeping our own instrument tuned and balanced (the subtle-energy equivalent of an actor's physical or vocal exercises), and also by helping us perceive and develop dramatic characters in more highly nuanced ways.

The seven major chakras (shown in Figure 3-1) are located, from bottom to top, at

1. the base of the spine
2. the lower abdomen or belly
3. the solar plexus
4. the heart (center of the chest)
5. the throat

6. the center of the forehead, just above and between the eyebrows ("third eye")
7. the crown of the head.

Each chakra has its own vibrational frequency, spinning slowly at the base of the spine and increasing in velocity while moving up the body-field. Each corresponds to specific organs, glands, and/or systems of the physical body; but most importantly for our work, each is aligned with specific aspects of our character.

There are numerous images and symbols to represent the chakras. In Hindu texts they're often pictured as lotus blossoms with a small number of petals on chakra 1 and increasingly more petals higher up. Often they're described as spinning vortices, like little whirlpools in water. Barbara Brennan, whose background is as a physicist, perceives them more scientifically than poetically, as cone-shaped funnels with their pointed tips at the center of the body-field and their open cone mouths reaching out from that center to the front and back edges of any given level of the field. I borrow her image for its simplicity and clarity (see Figure 3-2). The mouths of the cones face up, down, or to the front and back of the body to take in the surrounding energies. The small ends of the spinning cones open into a central channel which runs up and down the body parallel to the spine, into which the subtle energies travel to be released into the system, like water rising up from the roots of the tree and nourishment from the sun traveling down from the leaves.

Each chakra corresponds to and nourishes specific aspects of our being.

Chakra 1, the root chakra, is located at the base of the spine, its "mouth" pointing down toward the earth, and has the slowest vibration. It corresponds primarily to our sense of rootedness both on the earth and in our physical bodies, to the health of our physical selves, our will to live, our groundedness in the physical plane. It is associated with the element of earth.

Chakra 2 is in the center of the belly, the lower abdomen, and corresponds to the flow of emotion within us as well as to the quality and charge of our sexuality/sensuality. It has to do with inner fluidity and eros. Its element is water.

Chakra 3, at the level of the solar plexus, corresponds to our strength of will: our ability to take action in relation to our thoughts and dreams. In the physical body it feeds energy to the digestive system,

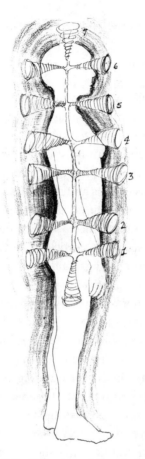

Figure 3-2. Side view of the chakras

and has to do with the metabolism of food as well as the mental and emotional absorption of thought and experience. Its element is fire.

Chakra 4, the heart chakra, is in the center of the chest at the level of the heart. It is at the center as well of this whole constellation of stars. Like Level 4 of the body-field, it is a bridge between the three chakras below and the three above. It corresponds to the strength and openness of our ability to love and be loved. Its element is air.

Chakra 5 is at the throat, and has to do both with our creativity and with speaking our truth. Speaking is usually thought of as the forming of words, but some people's truest communication comes through non-verbal expression: painting, music, dance, cooking, sports, and so forth. Significantly, it connects as well to our ability to *hear* the truth—in general and particularly about ourselves. Its realm is sound.

Chakra 6 is in the center of the forehead just above the eyebrows. Often called "the third eye," its power is of sight and insight—literal, metaphorical, and intuitive. In clairvoyants it is this center that is particularly charged. It corresponds to light.

Chakra 7, at the center of the top of the head, the crown, is our spiritual center. Not that the others are unconnected to spirit, but this energy center especially joins us to the spiritual forces beyond and around us. Its realm is ether.

These energy centers, as they run up the ladder from one to seven, are usually referred to as "lower" and "higher" because each successive chakra is of a higher frequency. The terms "lower and higher" could, given our conditioning, be taken to mean of lesser or greater value. Be careful. "Higher" here is not "better"—not unless you think that a tree's leaves are of higher value than its roots, or that adulthood is more important than childhood. All the chakras are of equal import within the functioning of the whole; they support each other, nourish each other, need each other for stability, vitality, and viability. As meditation teacher Jack Kornfield points out, you might go off to some mountaintop ashram for ten years and meditate yourself into a state of golden ether (higher frequencies), then come down the mountain into a traffic jam or the tangles of an intimate relationship and completely lose your marbles. What's below supports and sustains what's above; what's above feeds and illumines what's below.

This is not to say, of course, that in real people living through the vicissitudes of real life, much less characters undergoing the conflicts of a drama, that the energy centers will all be balanced, open, and superbly functioning or that they should be. The predilections, inclinations, strengths, and weaknesses we come in with rub up against the twists and turns of our story, shaping and being shaped by that story for better and for worse. Individual chakras can grow clearer and more vibrant through life. At times they can also become clogged, closed, frozen, or move into overdrive. They can leak out energy as if punctured by little holes, or take in too much energy and not know what to do with it. A chakra's dysfunction may be chronic or temporary. A blockage might have to do with a pattern of repeated life experiences or a harsh event that leaves a disruption in the energetic flow. Some conditions can be changed energetically, some may hold on forever.

There are times when what appears as dysfunction is a healthy and necessary condition for the moment. A healer perceiving someone's heart chakra as closed or weak would not automatically set out to heal it without understanding *why* an energy center is doing what it is. Maybe this person is in the painful throes of a divorce or has just lost a loved one, in which case it might be perfectly appropriate for that heart to protect itself for a while as it navigates the pain and, like any wound, take the time it needs to heal. Nor is it necessary to panic if you find out your root chakra is shut down. You might indeed have an illness or issues with being in your body; but you also might be in the middle of a move from one home to another, or be coming down with the flu, or have stubbed your toe five minutes ago. You may be able to tell, in other words, what's going on, but time is needed to understand the reasons for what you perceive.

On the other hand, a chakra may not, over time, be taking in or metabolizing the energy it needs to feed that part of the personality. This can happen for many reasons: genetics, birth and childhood experiences, illnesses, hurts or joys, failures or successes, obstacles in your path, family habits and patterns handed down, the condition of your environment, your relationships and all they entail. Conversely, the chakras' health or dysfunction affects many of those things in return—not genetics and heritage, of course, but most of the rest. Our personal story directly informs the state of our chakras, and the functioning of our chakras—as they inform our thoughts, actions, perspectives, abilities, feelings, body, and spirit—help to create our ongoing story.

Exercises 3 and 4 in Part II of this chapter are helpful for sensing and toning your energy centers, good for performers to do on a regular basis. Once you've got a sense of it, each takes about ten minutes and helps to keep your subtle instrument tuned, not only for entering character work, but offstage as well in the midst of a stressful and sometimes fickle profession. Doing them a few times a week is recommended until it becomes second nature. When developing character, you want to keep your own channels as clear, strong, and open as possible as a foundation onto which you add a few specific patterns of a character's energies, much as a strong and flexible physical body is the required base for an actor's portraying a character's physical qualities. As noted before, none of us is going to acquire a perfectly balanced chakra system exquisitely aligned at all times, which would actually be a disaster, an "Invasion of the Subtle-Body Snatchers." But clearing out what we don't need at any given time and strengthening the workings of the centers is simply cleaning house and won't turn us into interchangeable robots. Instead it can help us become a little more of exactly who we are to begin with.

You can usually tell a lot about a person's strongest chakras with clear vision and common sense. There are strong-willed people, deeply compassionate people, physically healthy and rooted people. There are those who are innately sensual, some whose rational intellects are literally shining, and some whose deep intuitive insight takes your breath away. No one's character is as simplistic as all that: a heart person, a body person, a truth-or-consequences person—but certainly these are touchstone qualities to perceive within the field. Knowing the condition of the chakras, especially those most vibrant, and tuning to their frequencies and qualities, is a way to embrace more of the essential hum of a character.

In acting training we learn to allow a free-flow of shifting emotion moment to moment, and so too we can adapt to the subtle energies' changing expression in response to the needs of the moment. Where we consciously use the energy field most in character work is in the basic palette of a character—a home base of finely threaded texture and hue. But a sensitivity to how the field shifts and pulses in the face of strong objectives, obstacles, or changing circumstances is always helpful.

Working with these energy centers is not all about softness, gentleness, and sweet little flows of golden light any more than life is. The women I worked with in postwar Bosnia had lost their husbands, sons, homes, possessions, professions, and any notion of what the future would hold. They'd seen torture and murder, endured rape, and had to attend exhumations of bodies at mass graves, hoping for a clue of a loved one's fate. Part of our daily workshops involved basic hands-on healing techniques which included, of course, work with the energy field. I was a bit nervous at raising the topic initially, but they took to it right away. "Oh!" they said. "The aura!" (They pronounced it ow-OO-ra.) "Yes, our grandmothers knew of this!" On my first visit, what was hardest for them in their state of post-traumatic stress, was grounding and centering. They had asked to be taught meditation to help with insomnia and anxiety, and I foolishly began with the usual foundation of rooting into the earth. But the earth for them was a place of battle, blood, and mass graves. I hadn't foreseen how terrible it would be for them to try to ground until I watched them trying to do it, growing rigid in their chairs, giggling sporadically, their breath shallow and erratic, their bodies resisting and rising up—anything to prevent that first chakra's opening and sending a root down into the chaos and misery of their land. The root chakra has to do with a sense not only of security in the physical body, but of one's sense of Home and well-being on the earth, all of which had been blasted by war, those foundational energy centers wounded in all of them. Energy, when it is cauterized or stopped from its flow for whatever reason, is no longer energy, as part of its definition is that *it is a current, it moves.* When it is ripped, blocked, or frozen, it becomes something else, for which there is no term, but which is definitely not something that feeds life. I learned very quickly to respect the collective condition of the women, understanding that any healing on this scale happens, if at all, only over a long period of time. We stopped the attempts to ground.

When I returned to Bosnia a year later, the women asked again for meditation instruction, eager to show what had shifted. Interestingly, most were able this time, without distraction or resistance, to root down into the earth. I do not know all the forces that helped them move forward, though the healing of the earth itself on which they walked, and the communal sharing of grief and mutual care had something to do with it. Nothing could ever bring back what was lost, relieve the anguish of what had been witnessed and experienced, eliminate the horror from their nights, or restore charmingly balanced chakra systems. But there was change. There was real modulation of energy and life-force, and the women were proud to be re-rooting into the earth as step-by-courageous-step they kept moving forward with their lives.

In a drama inspired by such situations, it's a performer's connection to this kind of vibrational reality that allows for the song of complexity to be singing beneath the words and illuminating the action. Finding one or two of such a field's notes to tune to—in this case both the specific design of pain as well as the fire and spiritual will to recover some of the strangled life-force, all expressed within the field—engenders richer character portrayal as well as a deepened sense of the given circumstances. (See Chapter 6 for more specificity.)

Finally, each chakra is associated with a color resembling its frequency. The color is not necessarily the color of the actual chakra according to those who see them clairvoyantly—but a correlating frequency to which that chakra also hums. Infusing your own energy centers with these colors charges up your own chakra constellation and can help you move deftly into the energy field of a character. The colors are easy to remember; from the bottom up, they follow the rainbow's spectrum.

Chakra 1: bright fire-engine red

Chakra 2: juicy orange

Chakra 3: lemon yellow

Chakra 4: leafy green

Chakra 5: rich royal blue

Chakra 6: indigo—the purple-blue of the night sky

Chakra 7: white

As with the exercise in *Clearing the Chakras,* toning with color (Exercise 4, Part II) is best done on a regular basis for meaningful results. Doing it twice a year is the same as turning up at the gym once every six months and expecting big results for your muscles.

From the preceding information you might begin to sort out which elements of your own field's levels and chakras are strong or fragile, and why you think so. Later, compare what you've deduced with your experiences of the exercises in the next section: What levels or energy centers are easy and fulfilling to enter? Which ones more difficult or initially frustrating? Some discoveries may be obvious, some surprising.

Very often you'll find yourself writing about or playing a character who has a weak energy center where yours is radiant, or a powerful one where yours is limp. There are a lot of things we can fake on stage with all manner of technique, but tuning to the energetic field isn't one of them. I once played a feisty German countess who'd been a member of the German anti-Hitler resistance and had saved countless souls in the war through a staggering force of wit and will. I met this woman in Berlin a few years before she died and have never encountered anyone with a more blazingly active third chakra (will). In portraying her, there were some of the usual acting leaps: body type and age, accent and voice, odd mannerisms, nothing unmanageable. What was hardest to achieve with integrity was her neon-yellow chakra 3. Just as with ongoing physical or vocal preparation for actors, we have to do a lot of work on ourselves with these energies: toning, empowering, and flexing our own subtle bodies through the exercises, but also through wrestling with our habitual perspectives and behaviors in real life, adding ever more color and texture and possibility to our own personal stories as we stretch to portray others'.

PAINTING THE BASE COAT[4]

Once, looking across a museum gallery at the portrait of a woman by Raphael, I was amazed by the glisten of realistic detail: the perfect sheen of satin folds, thick lustrous hair, the literal glow of the jewelry, the warm face of that one unique woman whose breathing aliveness, from across centuries and from out of a two-dimensional canvas, was so immediate and real. I walked close, expecting the illusion to fade, but even from three inches away the paint did not give itself away as paint nor would the technique show its face. The woman in the portrait and all her clothes and jewels were just as shimmering, substantial, and alive. I wished for x-ray vision, wondering with what magic base coat Raphael had brushed his canvas to bring it all to life with such textured radiance.

There are chakra clusters that, if their energies are running together with particular openness and power, point to a lifetime leaning in a given personality toward one of three qualities: reason, emotion, or will. To tune to one of these leanings is like applying such a base coat.

Healers learn to read the exact states of chakras and thus to calculate the force of the leanings. We do not need such precise skill, just (once again) clear observation, openness, and common sense to determine the leaning of a character or that of an individual on whom a character is based, to enter it on the subtle level and apply it as a base coat underlying the more intricate brush strokes of that portrayal.

We all know, for example, people whose power of clearly *reasoned thought* dominates their personalities; others who move from the wellsprings of the *heart*, and some with feisty and determined *wills*. No leaning is better than the others. Reason without heart, emotion with no reason, will without either, are nothing to aspire to. Most of us live with all three in a state of mutual support and interchange, yet also with an emphasis of one as a personal strength. We use that strength in exquisitely beautiful ways and also, in times of defensiveness or fear, will employ that same quality's negative face as protection or escape.

---

[4]Ibid. This section is based directly on Barbara Brennan's three modalities in *Hands of Light*, p. 73.

Looking again at Figure 3-2, note where the constellations fall. For each leaning, its particular group of chakras is generally running more energy in an individual than the other two groups.

Reason:
Chakra 6, front and back, and Chakra 7.

Emotion:
Chakras 2 through 5 along the front of the body.

Will:
Chakras 2 through 5 on the back of the body, as well as Chakra 1, pointing down to the earth.

Again, it's crucial not to confuse a general leaning for a grasp of the whole personality, leading to labeling and simplifying—the very flattening out of character we want at all costs to avoid: "Ah! He's a Reason Guy. She's an Emotion Lady!" If you use a leaning as entrance into character, use it only as a background wash onto which are painted all manner of unique details of that being's reality.

As for common sense and clear vision in determining someone's leaning without being able to read the chakras, just consider the people you know. In college I had a professor whose body hung loosely from the shoulders as if from a hanger. Joints loose, muscles slack, his strength was his mind, the energy around his head bright and exceptionally strong. He was not without heart or the will to accomplish what he needed to do— but thinking things out was his greatest delight: books, ideas, and research were his sport. A generally shy and kind soul, when up against a wall he could use his strength of reason in cool and manipulative ways.

You may know strong-willed people who have a dream, an idea, a goal, *and* the fire to accomplish it, no matter how difficult the task or how many tedious steps are required. Some are quiet, solitary sloggers who stick with the work till it's done to their taste; some are outspoken leaders and organizers, looked to for guidance by others. When countered or frightened or confused, their strong wills sometimes twist into an overload of control, domination, or resistance.

And then there are those who operate from the heart first. Generous, loving, delighted in the success of others, unabashedly sensitive to the emotional currents of whatever is happening, they can in good times be a source of compassion and sympathy, and in difficult situations, overemotional and unable to get a grip and move on. Or maybe one falls in love for the fiftieth time with the worst person imaginable, her heart on fire and her reason in a coma.

None of these leanings is inherently good, bad, or better than the others; they each need the others for support, shading, and essential sanity and can be used in both wonderful and less wonderful ways. And they are indeed base coats only, not a probing into the sharp-edged quirks and particulars of individual personality. But there are times when a conscious heightening of a leaning's chakra cluster can add extra resonance to a given characterization.

Exercise 5 in the next section helps you sense the leanings energetically.

After all these pages attempting to label the ineffable and organize the miraculous, the truth remains that the unending swirl of spirit into matter and matter into spirit and the infinite arabesques they make in the exchange is a mystery so vast we may never do more than stand on tiptoe peering over its windowsill into a few of its corners. The subtle body is only one of the dimensions of reality within which we live and through which we grow, relate, and change, each requiring a deepening of consciousness and encouragement of spirit. "If anything, subtle seems to be equivalent to fundamental. The effects of healing often seem to happen at a level below what scientists can comfortably measure right now. We do not yet have laboratory instruments that directly measure such qualities as love, desire or intention."[5] And yet, "such subtle influences may be more powerful than many more gross phenomena—in the same way that atomic energy in a few pounds of uranium has a lot more impact than a ton of TNT."[6]

Peter Brook has said that the art of theatre is to make the invisible visible. Who can count how many things that means or how many roads are traveled to find one's way into that territory? Still, as we straddle the visible and invisible every day of our lives and seek those graced moments of art where we might dance at the point of their meeting, the immeasurable rhythms of our subtle force fields are one winding road toward such a possibility.

---

[5]Goldner, Diane. 1999. *Infinite Grace: Where the Worlds of Science and Healing Meet.* Charlottesville, VA: Hampton Roads. p. 25.
[6]Ibid. p. 27.

PART II
Exercises
Exercise 1: Experiencing The Levels of the Field

This is a long exercise. When you have practiced it enough, you'll be able to move through it within seven to ten minutes, but at first it takes time as you learn to shift into each new vibration.

Make sure at the end of the exercise to work your way back down to level 1 and then into your physical body. Otherwise, you may go floating and flaking your way through the rest of the day.

You'll find some levels easier to experience than others. This does not mean that you are deficient, only that it's not easy to sense everything right away because, as noted a hundred times already, *it's subtle!* Also, all of us are more at home in some levels than others. Just pay clear attention to your experience at each stage, including when you're feeling pretty much nothing. Only when you've practiced repeatedly will the discrepancies in sensation begin to carry any meaning as to the real configurations of your own subtle body. The exercise asks you what it feels like at each step, but not what the feeling *means*. With practice, you'll be able to discern a pattern emerging of the levels you can tune to powerfully, and those which demand more time to come into.

Please read through the whole exercise before beginning, or tape it, or (if you're so blessed) have someone read you the instructions as you move along. This is to keep you from jumping back into your *thinking* mode (by furrowing your brow and reading the next instruction) as it's a non-rational state through which we sense the field.

Your mind's eye or imagination is a doorway through which the rest of the sensation can enter. Move from image to other modes of perceiving throughout your body and five senses. Make sure you keep your breath easy and deep in your belly. The quality of breath is very important here. No controlling or forcing of it; just check in on it from time to time, and root it gently down to your center, staying grounded throughout.

- Standing or seated, center and ground.
- Breathe easily, make sure your pelvis is loose. Think of something to make you smile, even laugh, to relax the whole system. If you go into this with steely jaws of determination, you'll stop breathing, have a hard time sensing, and even if you feel it, one wonders what for.

- Relax your eyes' focus.
- Imagine that hugging your whole body is a light blue network of softly pulsing light lines, interwoven in a finely meshed grid. If it takes some time to establish this image in your mind's eye, so be it. Stay with level 1 for a moment or two, trying to sense its subtle pulse around every part of your body, noting how it makes you feel. This is the level of being at home in your physical self and on the earth.
- With imagination and intention, expand the field outward two or three inches, and perceive it now as melting away from the structured grid to a formless flow of fine cloudlike substances—all the colors of the rainbow's spectrum: red, orange, yellow, green, blue, violet, and white—floating around and through your physical body. This is the level of free-flowing emotions. What does it make you feel? Stay with it a few moments, noticing the quality of the colors: Dim? Blackish? Bright and clear?
- Move to level 3, extending even farther outward in a shining, glimmering yellow grid of pulsating light lines. Feel the clarity of this level, its etched, cut-glass refinement. This is the level of your analytical mind, your intellectual focus, curiosity and probing acuteness. How does the sensation of this level contrast with the one before? Is it difficult or easy for you to imagine and maintain? Note when there is a struggle and when there is a relaxing into any given level. No need for judgment about perceived strengths or weakness, just focused observation.
- Expand now to level 4, the level of relational loving, of the heart. Here is another unstructured and cloudlike realm, expanding out to about a foot from your skin, its rainbow colors infused with a rosy glow as if the red, orange, yellow, green, blue, and violet of the spectrum are seen through rose-colored glasses. Feel the delicate floating clouds carrying the feeling of love in all its many aspects—not only of the capacity to give love and compassion but also, very significantly, to receive and assimilate it. Think of something or someone you love deeply—a person, a pet, a landscape, an exquisite piece of music—and let that connection inform the shapes and colors of this fluid level. How does it feel? Is this level a struggle or a joy? Note its difference from the level preceding it. Stay there for a few moments.

- Opening further now to an even higher frequency of your subtle body, move to level 5—the attunement of your own will to a higher will, the meshing of your direction with the path (whether in the moment or in the long term) you were meant for. You might imagine it as a thick grid of shining silvery-white light lines out to about one and one-half feet from your body, buzzing on an invisible grid of great magnitude which extends so far out you cannot see it; you can only sense the entrainment of the two hums: yours and the greater will. You might, on the other hand, feel more comfortable imagining it as a grid of negative space, like the negative of a photograph, sitting in a rich field of cobalt blue, whichever works best for you. As you expand into this level of empowered will, having more to do with surrender than force or brute stubbornness, notice if it is a struggle for you to move into this state, if you can begin to manage it but only weakly, if it pops in fiercely, if it's somewhere in the middle.

- Through your intention and imagination, expand outward farther (to two to two and one-half feet) to the sixth level of unconditional love of all things. This is different from level 4, a more earthed and humanly fallible level where you get to pick and choose what you love, and when and why. On level 6 it is a more encompassing love—the kind we may experience at the exquisitely heightened moments of our lives: the births, the deaths, the fallings in love. This fluidly moving, nonstructured level of loving with the deepest and most eternal part of ourselves is lit again by the colors of the rainbow, but in this case they are more delicate and glowing with the shimmer of mother-of-pearl. Note how you feel in this space and if it is one you prefer to stay within or to exit.

- Allow one last expansion through your intention and imagination to the seventh level of the subtle body: radiant and glimmering golden light lines in a tight pulsing weave of dancing interchange. This is the last structured level. It extends at least three feet from your physical self and, in interpenetrating all the others, contains all of you within it. It integrates body, emotion, will, heart, higher will, higher love, and spirit in its shimmering matrix. It connects you to the life-force outside your own boundaries and holds your own music in the embrace of the all-encompassing mystery. How does it feel?

- Now, step-by-step, move your way back down the levels, all the way back to your physical body, your material self in this moment. At each step downward, breathe out the expanded state that you are in, and visualize moving down to the level below it. Breathe it in, then breathe out that level, and move down all the way to level 1. Breathe out the first level from your consciousness, come into your physical body, and stretch gently all over. Re-ground, open your eyes, and take stock of the whole trip.

Practice. And practice again. There's no speedy MacEnergy-Field way to acquire a clear hold on these different states of being and perceiving. Eventually, however, you will be able to slide easily in and out of most of these frequencies and use that ability when interviewing people for your work, when preparing to go on stage, and when portraying a character.

Exercise 2: Energetic Boundaries

The first section of this exercise is inspired by and adapted from the work of Andrea Olsen and Caryn McHose in *Body Stories*.[7]

A. Cellular Awareness

- Lie on your back with the soles of your feet on the floor, knees up and resting against one another. Let your arms relax on the floor at an angle from your torso. Breathe into your belly.
- Imagine yourself as a single cell. Feel the boundary of the outer membrane. Be aware of yourself contained, as a single unit, with all parts of your body contributing to the whole, and safe within a clear, defining cell wall. Breathe into this individuated containment for a few moments.
- Now imagine briefly that this cell wall is made of bricks and mortar. Nothing can enter into or leave through this thick barrier; it's you on one side of it and everything else on the other. Five seconds of this is enough, but in that brief time, notice how it makes you feel.

---

[7]Olsen, Andrea, and McHose, Caryn. 1991. *Body Stories*. Barrytown, New York: Station Hill Press.

- Shift the image of the cell wall to a porous mesh, allowing for an exchange with the world around you, the mesh preventing the entrance of what does not belong inside. Stay for a few moments with a sense of flowing interchange between inside and out.

B. *Subtle Boundary Awareness*

- Continuing in the same relaxed position, expand your awareness as far as you can out from your skin to the edges of your subtle body. This might be three inches for now; it might be three feet, no matter. With your intention, clarify and sharpen the sense of your field's boundary, the edge of your unique self holding the floating maps of your story.
- At first, imagine it as a closed and rigid membrane all around you, protecting and separating you from the flow of life. Don't hold this very long, just for a quick sense of what it feels like in whatever shape and form it comes to your mind's eye: a wall, a suit of armor, a thick shell . . . Notice what is not allowed in, and what cannot get out. Notice how it makes you feel.
- Now shift your awareness of the outer membrane and envision it as a clear, pulsing, and definable boundary, but made of subtle, shifting, gently vibrating energies able to *exchange streams of energetic force* with the outer world. How does it feel?
- Imagine your whole self as a cell again, but this time as a cell inside an enormous body within which you are one tiny part. Your boundary is still permeable, allowing energies in and easing them out.
- After a few moments, let it go, relax, breathe into your physical body and stretch.

Exercise 3: *Clearing the Energy Centers or Chakras*

- Sit comfortably with closed eyes, the soles of your feet on the floor, your back straight but not rigid. Move through the exercise with focus and care. If your attention wanders, gently refocus it without yelling at yourself.
- Center and ground, gently rooting your breath.

- Imagine a waterfall of light coming down from the sky—from a star, the moon, the sun, or beyond. It beams down toward the crown of your head.
- Focus your attention on the crown chakra (#7). Breathe into a sphere, a few inches in diameter, that surrounds and radiates from the crown. With each breath let the sphere fill with warmth and a soft golden or white light. Imagine that any debris, clogging, heaviness, or old garbage cluttering that space is being released on each outbreath. Inhale clear light, exhale a gray mist of whatever might be obstructing this center. Continue for a few breaths, your attention focused, until you get the sense of the brightening and warming and clearing of this center.
- Let the beam of light stream down from the crown to chakra 6, between the eyebrows in the center of the head. Again, envisioning a sphere surrounding that space, and with the *intention* of clearing that energy center, breathe in clear light and imagine breathing out a dull brown mist taking with it any obstructions. Continue for several breaths. Then place your attention on both chakras 6 and 7, feeling the clarity of both.
- Imagine the light sinking downward to your throat chakra (#5). Repeat the process, breathing in warm clear light, breathing out the dull mist, until you feel the throat area cleared and softly lit.
    (These dull mists won't pollute the air around them. They're absorbed and transformed into clear energy.)
- Move the light downward as before through the central channel connecting the energies of all the field's centers to the heart chakra (#4) in the center of the chest, clearing it in the same way for several slow, easy breaths. Again, for each energy center, imagine clearing a spherical space both within and around that center.
- Then let the waterfall of light sink down to the third chakra at the solar plexus, breathing and clearing gently as before, staying with it for a few breaths.
- Down to the second chakra, carrying the line of clear light through the central channel and clearing this energy center with the same soft breaths, staying with it for a few moments.
- And finally, let the current of light through the channel all the way down to chakra 1 at the base of the spine, opening to a sense of that sphere and cleaning it out in the same relaxed way with your attention, intention, and breath.

- Once you have moved through all the chakras, see if you can expand your attention to include them all. Breathe the light into all seven at once, see in your mind's eye their being connected by a central channel of light running up and down your body-field, breathe out any remaining mist or remains of old blocked debris.
- Sense your roots in the ground once more, then stretch and open your eyes. Note how you feel.

Exercise 4: Strengthening the Chakras Through Color

The most important thing in this practice is to step beyond merely *thinking the color in your mind*, which will affect very little. You need to *become* the color throughout the cells of your whole body. You want to feel that color's rhythm, density, temperature, scent, and/or taste as you match its frequency. There are a couple of ways to help you get there written into the instructions below. Try them both and see which works best for you.

You will notice as you move through the colors that some are easier to tune to than others. Like the levels of the field, you'll struggle with some (too pale, too dark, too irritating to deal with), while you slide easily and pleasurably into others. No judgment necessary. You are not broken, and the exercise isn't sadistic. First, it takes time to get used to the exercise, and it may have to do with the moment in time. But mostly, all of us have both stronger and weaker energy centers as well as the qualities to which they correspond. It took me (sigh) ten years to achieve a really bright yellow for my own third chakra. That's the way we are.

- Sit comfortably with a straight spine. Center, ground, and breathe.
- Set your attention on the root chakra at the base of your spine. Now imagine that a giant bucket of bright red paint, a few feet above your head, is being poured onto and all through your body. All of you *becomes* this rich, bright red: your bones, tissues, muscles, blood, organs, glands, skin, and hair and the field around you. What does it feel like? Is it hot or cold? Dense or fine? Can you smell it? Taste it?

   Now focus your attention specifically on the area of and around your root *chakra* again. Imagine that all the red throughout your body is feeding, filling, and radiating from this center. Hold that state and its sensation for a few moments.
- Allow the red to rise up through the central energetic channel parallel to your spine till it reaches the center of your lower

abdomen, the second chakra. As it rises, visualize the color transmuting from red to *bright orange*. Imagine that the nuclei of all the cells of your body are filled with this orange, the color radiating into the whole of each cell and suffusing it with its scent, rhythm, density, temperature, taste—whatever qualities come with it for you. While your whole body is infused with orange, focus it especially on the area of chakra 2. Note if it's bright and clear or in some way muted. Don't judge or strain for what's not there—just pay attention to the quality you actually sense. Stay with it for a few moments, breathing easy, seeing how you feel within it, then move on.

- Let the flood of orange rise up to chakra 3 at your solar plexus transmuting on the way into *bright yellow*. Choose one of the two ways to infuse your whole body with bright sunrise yellow (the bucket of paint being poured over your whole system, or the color emanating from the nuclei of every cell) and then focus it especially on your solar plexus. How difficult or easy is it to become this color? How does it make you feel? What sensations does it engender? Hold it, filling up the chakra with this vibration, then move up to chakra 4.

- The yellow changes to a rich, springtime, leafy *green* as it approaches the heart chakra in the middle of your chest. Let your body fill with the green in whichever way works best for you. Then, setting your attention particularly on the heart area with green filling and radiating from it, take note of what it feels like to *become* that color. Hold for a few moments in chakra 4, breathing the color in and out, and move on.

- Rising from the heart chakra to chakra 5 at the throat, the green turns into *royal blue*, filling your whole body, and especially the throat. Breathe the color in, breathe the color out; become the vibration of royal blue and note how it makes you feel. Stay with it for a few moments, imagining that blue to be as deep and as sapphire-like as possible, and get ready for a leap downward.

- To check out the different sensations of each color vibration, jump back down now to chakra 1 at the root of the spine, and fill it and your whole body again with *red*, remembering not just to think the red but to become its essence. Do you feel a difference in quality between the sensations of royal blue and bright red? If not, you may just be imagining the colors in your head and not tuning to each distinctive frequency. If you do, you're on the right track. What's the difference in sensation? Now leap up to green at the heart, and see if there's another shift in your sensation. Then rise back to the throat's blue. Hold and breathe there for a moment, and then rise to chakra 6.

- As you visualize the color rising up from the throat to the middle of the forehead, let the blue deepen to a dark *purple-blue indigo*, like the midnight sky. Sense how this color, filling your whole body and especially your upper head, makes you feel; be as precise as you can about the sensory qualities it stimulates in you. Is it easy to move into? Difficult? Calming? Annoying? Just note it, breathe, hold it, and move on.

- As the indigo rises up to the crown of the head, it transmutes to white. Every cell of your body is radiant with this clear white, flooding through and around your whole system, fountaining out of your crown chakra down the front, back, and sides of your body, all the way to the ground. All of you is white, but your attention now is most powerfully on the chakra 7 at the crown. Stay here a few moments, and note as specifically as you can how it makes you feel.

- Now move back down the spectrum from chakra 7 all the way down to the root chakra, stopping very briefly at each center to attend to the sensation of its color, and holding and charging each one for a moment. *White* at the crown, *indigo* at the center of the forehead, *blue* at the throat, *green* at the heart, *yellow* at the solar plexus, *orange* at the center of the pelvis, and *red* at the base of the spine.

- After a few more breaths at chakra 1, reestablish your roots in the earth down from your belly center and from the soles of your feet. Stretch slowly, open your eyes, and sit quietly for a moment, taking stock of what the experience was like and what you feel right now.

Exercise 5: The Three Leanings

The core of this exercise is to be done as you move through the day from one activity to another, rather than sitting down quietly and meditating on it. To prepare for it, however, first practice the sense of each leaning:

- *For reason:* Charge the three head chakras (chakra 7, plus the front and back of chakra 6) first just by setting your attention on them clearly, and then sending energy up there, imagining all three energy centers to be radiant with pulsing light. Visualize your whole head and the field around it as golden and buzzing with aliveness. You do not have to pretend to be smarter or more intellectual than you are; let go of any expectations and modifiers. Just focus on the light and the sense of soft energetic activity around your head, and set your intention on those chakras being open to a healthy exchange—in and out—of *prana*.

- *For emotion*: Do the same sequence with chakras 2 through 5 *on the front* of your body-field.
- *For will*: The same again with chakra 1, and chakras 2 through 5 *on the back* of your body-field.
- In all three cases, let your imagination and intention help create the reality, if only momentarily, that one of these qualities at a time—reason, emotion, or will—is your greatest strength, the place from which you move, work, daydream, play, love.

The rest of the exercise is more of an arpeggio, in that it can be done repeatedly and at various times throughout your day. Try it with each of the three leanings.

- Whatever you're doing—cooking a meal, reading a book, speaking to a friend, shopping for groceries, sewing a rip in your pants, preparing a role—try the action from within the base coat of one particular leaning or another, and notice how each informs your relation to yourself and whatever you're engaged in doing. Let the qualities of each lead you through your activities, setting the tone of behavior, perspective, and how you approach each situation and initiate each action.
- Note if there are times when a quality you're emphasizing comes out felicitously, or when it feels too strong or awkward, when it helps and when it hinders, when it expands or contracts your way of thought, feeling, or action. Notice its effects on others: Does it open or close them when you are using this leaning as a base coat? With which leanings do you feel uncomfortable? With which at ease?

This last exercise does not need to be done more than once, but the other four need to be done again and again to build the muscle for shifting in and out of the different states swiftly, strongly, and clearly.

4

CHAPTER

Listening

A WAY OF HOSPITALITY

In the world of quantum physics there's no such thing as an objective observer of a thing; rather, the nature and definition of what is being observed is determined by who is perceiving it, and when, and under what circumstances. As a result, what we'd thought of as an observer is actually a *participant* in the definition of what is being perceived.

It is the same with observing or listening to a story. How it is expressed depends profoundly on how it's being heard. How it breathes, speaks, and moves its limbs alters in accordance with who is listening and with what manner of attention. There's an elegance to fine listening, a graciousness which sinks us further down into our shared humanity.

As actors and writers we strive to take in people's stories with more than ears and intellect, for the integrity of our listening informs directly the quality and interchange of energies between listener and speaker, and therefore the nature of the story being told. The content of a story is of course what it is, but its resonance, its flavor, the vistas it will open to, the layering of how it is spoken, and the relation of teller to story in that moment of telling, has everything to do with how it's being heard. The hearing rests in how we hold our own invisible fields, what energies we charge or relax as we listen, how we "hold the ground" for a speaker, what our *intention* in listening is to begin with, and always the state of our heart.

As Buddhist monk Thich Nhat Hanh writes,

When we want to understand something, we cannot just stand outside and observe it. We have to enter deeply into it and be one with it in order to really understand. ... The word *comprehend* is made up of the Latin roots *com,* which means "to be one with," and *prehendere,* which means "to grasp it or pick it up." Therefore, to comprehend something means to pick it up and be one with it. There is no other way to understand something. You have to enter to be one with what you want to observe and understand."[1]

ARPEGGIOS: "LISTENING" FOR THE EFFECTS OF LISTENING

- Note the state of your subtle energies when you are half-listening to someone else. Are they pulling away from the other person? Shutting down? Straining? Flying off in all directions? Thinning out? Filled with your own noise? Which of your own chakras seem open or closed?
- Sense what happens to your field when you are listening wholly and fully. Is it bright or dim? Large or contracted? Rooted or not? What chakras seem open or closed?
- Note your physical and subtle energetic responses at those times when you yourself are being listened to half-heartedly, and at those other times when you are being heard with depth and expansiveness.

Many of us learned in public school a kind of consumer listening: taking in just what will serve our own agenda and get us the good grades. When I was a school kid, we sat in those long, alphabetical rows of desks. The teacher would ask a question, and half of us would fling hands in the air, waving wildly for attention. A lot of us didn't know the answer but wanted some attention. When Dwight or Sally were called on, our listening to *them* was not the point, not how we got our gold stars and praise. They talked, we kept our hands flying like flags in the air. It's hard for a teacher to gauge the quality of students' silences anyway; our rewards usually came from spouting out what we could.

---

[1]Thich Nhat Hanh. 1988. *The Heart of Understanding.* Berkeley: Parallax Press. p. 11.

Later we grow up using the same skills: mentally highlighting and underlining those things another says that we can use in our books, promotions, sales pitches, or power plays, hijacking selected bits of useable content and dismissing the overall context, the relationship of what is spoken to who is speaking it, losing a sense of all that's *not* being spoken, or the mystery and unique music of the speaker himself. Somewhere along the way we came to believe that speaking is active and powerful, listening passive and wimpy, and that the speakers are the leaders and the listeners mere followers. But the power of fine listening is an active and evocative force unto itself.

When listening to a story, whether through an interview or other circumstances, we can absorb the telling in two ways: (1) for the meaning and style of the words themselves, but also (2) for the voice, body, spirit, soul, rhythm, texture, and the flow of subtle energies, all parts of the story's body too. We can take it in like music, letting it have its unique effect not only on minds and hearts, but also on our bodies, force fields, spirits.

Exercise: Listening to Music

- Choose at least five CDs or cassette tapes with contrasting musical selections. You might choose a lively Klezmer song, then the Kyrie of Mozart's Requiem, a slow and sultry Muddy Waters, a fugue from Bach's *Well-Tempered Clavier*, Tuvan throat singers, some thumping, swinging gospel. You'll play about three minutes of each selection.
- After you put each piece of music onto the CD/cassette player, lie down on your back, knees in the air, soles of your feet on the floor, and breathe deeply into your body from toes to head. Focus your attention, and set your intention to listen with your entire body-field.
- Let the music come into your cells, riding in on your breath right through your skin, into your bones and muscles, the thrum of your heart and blood, all of you. What specifically does it make you feel? How does the music change your inner rhythm, your perspective, your subtle body's patterning and pace? How does it touch your body, heart, and/or spirit? If some selections make you want to get up and move or dance, go for it. Remember that music is vibration moving through your field, which itself is vibration.
- After a few minutes of each piece, change to the next selection, lying down again and letting the next kind of music soak right into your body-field. Ask the questions above with each piece.

- Note the varied effects of different music on your being, as well as how quickly and fluidly your energies change in their responses from one kind of vibration to another.

When, through distraction and half-hearted listening, we miss the *music* of a teller and her tale, when unconsciously, through inner clutter or too narrow a focus, we prevent its entering, moving through, and even changing us, we miss some of the story's spirit, miss the song at the core, we may miss the point.

There are cultural habits and patterns which relentlessly nudge us away from true listening. Sogyal Rinpoche, in *The Tibetan Book of Living and Dying* describes both Eastern and Western styles of what he calls "spiritual laziness." Western laziness, he writes, "consists of cramming our lives with compulsive activity so that there is no time at all to confront the real issues." In our country, in these times, four variations on the theme of "cramming" are *stress, pressure, speed* and *noise*, each of which has specific effects on our physical and subtle bodies that spin us away from clear perception, twisting and muddying the lucidity with which we hear, and therefore the soul of *what* we hear.

Stress involves the overwhelm of too-muchness: the too-many things we juggle in a day, and the countless fragments of information we are expected to make sense of. We jam our days with to-do lists and make sure our lives are crowded enough to assure we're not killing time or wasting our lives. It isn't the idea of stress per se that's unnerving; we all need a certain amount of stress to function at all in our lives, as a rubber band needs to be stretched to be useful. It's only when that rubber band is stretched to a point of *dis-stress* that it weakens and snaps. On the highway, when there's construction work with those thick cement barriers narrowing the road, we instinctively slow down to navigate the squeezed lane more sanely. Curiously, we don't always translate that instinct into the narrowed lanes of our overcrowded lives: instead of slowing down, we usually speed up to get it all done, and we crash.

One of the main effects of stress on our subtle bodies is to *push our breath and energy up out of our centers, into our shoulders, necks, heads, and beyond, uprooting us, pulling us up off the ground like a plug yanked out of its socket, disconnected from the juice.*

Pressure, a first cousin to stress, is about having (or believing we have) too little time. Though we may be extraordinarily patient in the long haul, in the immediate haul, we're usually rushing or ruled by strict time limits for doing this or that before the next task rings the doorbell and demands entrance.

The effect of pressure on our subtle energies is that *we become constricted.* Our field literally *contracts. We pull in.* Sometimes the energy *stiffens,* like there's too much starch in it. Or *we harden our boundaries* and cut ourselves off from an intake of *prana.*

Speed. The fact that we live fast-paced lives is a cliché, but there we are. We consume books and workshops about time management and strive to be efficient, as if it's right up there with the most important qualities in the world. (Woody Allen said, "Yes, I took a speed-reading course. I read *War and Peace.* It's about Russia.") We clock our drives to see how fast we can make it to Minneapolis from Denver. When stuck in a traffic jam, we can feel our subtle bodies pushing so far out of our physical selves—which are trapped in the car which is trapped in the jam—that it's as if part of us is smashing against the windshield, banging to get out.

It seems we are deemed worthier and more effective the faster we can accomplish something—setting deadlines that fly in the face of going deeply into a given project or allowing for real innovation and risk. "In our society," writes Jerry Mander,

> speed is celebrated as if it were a virtue in itself. ... The true result has been an increase in human anxiety, as we try to keep up with the growing stream of information. Our nervous systems experience the acceleration more than our intellects do. It's as if we're all caught in a socially approved video game, where the information on the screen comes faster and faster as we try earnestly to keep up.[2]

As far as listening is concerned, speed sucks the blood right out of it. I used to pontificate to my academically pressured students on the *time* real artistic discovery requires, begging them to give themselves the room for it. They'd crowd round me after class, relieved at the whole notion of slowing down, wanting to come to my office and talk

---

[2]Mander, Jerry. 1991. *In the Absence of the Sacred: The Failure of Technology and the Survival of the Indian Nations.* San Francisco: Sierra Club Books. p. 64.

further. And I, gripped by "the Reality Police" as a friend calls it, would glance wildly at my watch. "Well, we have to make it fast; I have three committee meetings, two advisees coming in, and a rehearsal. How about we take three minutes here in the hall?"

The effect of the speed in our lives is to *push our subtle bodies forward out of our physical selves, straight into the windshield, sometimes crashing right through. Energetically we start walking ahead of ourselves, our fields literally half-in and half-out.*

Finally, *Noise*. Not natural sounds. *Noise.* We have bravely adapted to it as if the intrusion of unwanted noise were a natural part of life, like the weather. (I read somewhere that Lily Tomlin is worried that the guy who invented Muzak is coming up with a new invention.) There's all the outer noise, the lawn mowers, leaf blowers, hedge clippers, truck engines, and low-flying planes; and there's the inner noise that comes in part from stress, pressure, and speed.

Noise grabs our subtle bodies by the neck, turns them upside down and jangles them every which way. *Our fields lose coherence, fluidity, and calm; they bounce around erratically; they go haywire.*

It isn't that I imagine some paradise where there were no such forces working against us and that poor us, we live in hell on earth: "Oh if only we could go back to the good old days of the Depression or the Black Plague or the Inquisition or the Crusades and then, *then,* we'd all be able to listen deeply." No. Just that where we are now does have its own peculiar and idiosyncratic currents that pull us away from firm shore. And to listen well, the first thing we need is to feel on solid ground. And if we don't find it in the rushing river we're in, we need to make an island of that ground within us.

So here are our subtle bodies on a daily basis flying off in all directions without our thinking twice about it—*up and out* from stress, into *contraction* from pressure, *forward and out* from speed, *scattered and jangled* from noise—all conditions that prevent us from seeing or listening to others and the world around us at a level of actual connection. Instead, we become fabulously adept at a slick, consumer perception, an efficient, compact listening for a double-speed, overcrowded life.

Something of beauty, delicacy, even passion gets lost in the crush, something to do with the *spirit* of story as it's offered and received. The possibility of communion and comprehension sneaks out the back door and skulks away. And inevitably, the superficiality of the taking in will be reflected in one's writing and the ultimate performance. But:

We can make our minds so like still water that beings gather about us, that they may see their own images, and so live for a moment with a clearer, perhaps even with a fiercer, life because of our quiet.

—*W.B. Yeats*

If we wanted, we could build a house of our listening. A house welcoming and hospitable so that a story, which has a body and a life of its own, could walk in and settle down. A house with wide doorways, open windows, sturdy walls, light and warmth inside, an absence of clutter, sitting on a firm foundation, solid ground. The ground is made of *stillness, silence* and *spaciousness.*

When I suggest this possibility in workshops, some people burst out laughing, some go glazed-eyed, and some heave a two-pound sigh from their thighs. One woman said, "Great. Fine. What planet are you suggesting we move to?"

No other planet, just that little house.

Stillness would ask that we stop the forward push, the juggling of many thoughts and tasks, the inner buzz of striving to *accomplish* something this minute, and just be present. I don't mean in general, and from here to eternity, although if you can do that, fabulous. I mean rooted for this moment, or hour, of listening.

Silence is of course about shutting the window to the weed whackers and snowblowers, but also about dimming the noise in our heads— of the critic, the editor, the father figure, the nurse, the nag, the guru, the devil's advocate, the worrywart—internal voices like so many jackhammers obliterating the integrity of someone else's (not to mention our own) story.

Spaciousness is a form of respect. It grants that not only does a person have a body, but so does her story, which needs room to breathe, spread its legs, find its true note. Spaciousness doesn't mean moving from the Bronx to the Catskills. It means giving both the person inside the story and the story inside the person a place to root and time to sprout.

It might be noisy and pressured all about you, it might be mayhem. You learn to make it otherwise inside. Once, in an overcrowded refugee camp in the West Bank, I interviewed a Palestinian woman as we stood on the rubble of her home, bulldozed to the ground that morning by the Israeli army. Scores of people were walking by in the midst of their own loud conversations; the woman's seven children were at our feet, crying, and playing with sling-shots; more bulldozers were at work not far away.

The woman herself, panicked about finding another place for her children to live, was screaming her story at me in a red-hot rage. "You're a Jew? Look what you did to my home! What are we supposed to do now? What is the matter with you?" It was not what you'd call a still, silent, or spacious interviewing venue. In these situations there is no time or place for long, deep meditations and preparation. It must happen instantly, and as with all such skills, it comes from practicing in advance, until you can build your listening house in two seconds' time when needed.

Learning some form of meditation cannot hurt. There are many kinds: walking meditation, dancing meditation, seated-on-a-cushion-being-still meditation, leaning-against-a-tree-listening-to-the-sounds-of-the-woods meditation. But this is not a meditation manual; that worthy practice is something to pursue on your own if you are so moved, to strengthen your attentive muscle.

For here, you can build such a listening house energetically by

- rooting into the earth (centering and grounding),
- setting your intention to be present and receptive,
- clearing and expanding your energy field (through focused intention), and
- consciously strengthening your heart.

The discussion and exercises in this chapter speak of listening in relation to receiving literal stories as spoken to you. They reflect my own bent toward and experience with interviewing people of all kinds in many situations. I go with a tape recorder, seek out people, and make appointments for speaking together—but none of that may be your way. The listening of which I speak includes taking in all kinds of stories, including those that have no words, and is relevant to almost all modes of gathering material. It applies as well to watching a person; to hearing a fragment of something on the off chance with no scheduled meeting or tape machine; to tasting the food of a feast of foods you've never tried before; to absorbing the behavior, shape, and mannerism of humans and other creatures, or a city's idiosyncratic bustle, sound, and rhythm. It is a listening that opens wide to bearing witness to all the features and the finest hairs of a story's face.

Exercise: Building a Listening House

[Note: You will find that with this and subsequent exercises, you need to practice first the exercises in Chapter 3 that give you the foundation you'll need to manage work with individual chakras or the field as a whole. So be it. Go back to that "warehouse" as needed, take from its shelves the relevant practices, and strengthen your energetic muscles in your own time.]

- Center and ground.
- Set your "roots" very firmly in the earth, and imagine yourself "holding the ground"—which means maintaining a steady rootedness no matter what the circumstances—for whatever emerges to be truly welcomed. There is an art to hospitality. It has been cultivated to exquisite form in countries of the Middle East, for example, where one learns ways of welcome that are not nurtured in our own rushed and atomized society.

Once, in the Syrian desert, some friends and I stopped at a Bedouin home to ask if we could see something on their land. A breathtakingly beautiful Bedouin woman answered the door, an infant in her arms, more tiny children clutching at her long skirts. She stared at our clearly American selves for a moment, gasped, and broke into a radiant smile. "Strangers!!" she called in unabashed delight to her relatives in the compound. "Oh come see! Strangers!" And to us: "Halloo!" which meant, *Change your direction. Please! Stop here! Come this way!* Never had I experienced more spontaneous joy at one's being confronted by strangers. Not only an absence of suspicion or fear, but a fascinated wonder at what the encounter might hold and what hospitality she might offer. Imagine if we opened our door in this way to a new and strange story: "Halloo! Stop here. Come this way!"

- Open your field: visualize it expanding, clearing, and brightening, using a marriage of intention and imagination to effect it. This may take some time as you get started; with practice it takes seconds. It's partly the clarity of focus that matters, and partly *the sincerity of the intention.* There is no way of faking energetic shifts; your true thoughts are energy patterns themselves and will be right there in the flow at all times.
- Open your heart chakra. Begin with *the intention* that it be open, and setting your attention on the heart, imagine running clear energy through it. To help the opening,
  - think of someone or something you dearly love,
  - fill chakra 4 with rich forest green, or
  - fill it with a rich rose color.

- With attention and intention, open the fourth level of your field. Using the fourth chakra as a gateway into the fourth level, visualize that level's qualities and essence, and then open the visualization to include your other senses.
- Practice when listening to anyone or anything. Notice when you become distracted, filled with your own noise, or want to interrupt unnecessarily. Practice clearing your field quickly again (and again) with your intention, breathing in clear light, breathing out a dusty mist of any clutter, expanding your field, centering and grounding again. Remember the idea of a house with its firm foundation and clear space into which you are welcoming a guest.
- As you listen, absorb the music of both story and teller and, with curiosity rather than judgment, note its effects on you. Remember that the story and the voice are alive and shaped within that person's subtle energies which are having a direct impact for better or for worse on your own.

Please note: The point is not to *indicate* listening, one smarmy style involving nodding your head all the time to point out how much you care, furrowing your brow to prove that you're concentrating, and saying "I hear you," or "Thank you for sharing" in a throaty voice. Better you should be completely rude and obnoxiously inattentive; at least it's honest.

Stillness, silence and spaciousness will not be handed to you on a silver salver at the door of an interview, and rarely anywhere else. You'll find yourself listening in all manner of unusual and challenging situations; the reality of the environment often becomes part of the vitality of the story and eventually even of the monologue.

Sometimes you will need to take stock of the state of the speaker's energy field and use your own to stabilize, tune to, or balance it according to the need of the moment (i.e., opening your field into a warm, bright state when the speaker is having a hard time with what's being said, matching their great expansiveness with your own expanded energy, visualizing cooling colors of the field—such as blue or green— if the storyteller's energies are getting overheated). From time to time check your own energies to see if they've become frozen, stuck, disconnected, or sluggish.

Never use your own energy field to manipulate the speaker's—as in, "Oh God, he's too angry; I'll calm my field and tone him down," or, "My goodness, so much pain! I'll expand and brighten my field to perk her right up!" Heaven forbid. Just make more *room* for the anger or pain, and hold your own energy steady, grounded, and clear so that another's honest emotions, whatever they may be, have room to breathe and firm ground to stand on. It is not necessary or wise to merge with the speaker's feelings, taking them into yourself and collapsing under the weight of them. Simply keep clearing away your own muck, admitting whatever comes, and respecting it on its own terms.

On the other hand, when interviewing, while you don't want to reject or manipulate the story's life, you also don't want to leave your interviewee in a fractured or distressed state. Make sure that you help close the door of an interview graciously, with the quiet toning, balancing, and rooting down of your own field, never leaving precipitously once you've "got what you want."

INCLUSIVE ATTENTION

In the world of healing, healers practice a kind of listening or lucid perception which connects the healer's own energy with that of the client deeply and noninvasively in order to "hear" or perceive the condition of the client's subtle energies. (With healers, perception occurs often through the hands.) Healer Susan Borg calls this connective awareness "inclusive attention," which is a helpful description of what we're doing when we listen to story. It's a focused and expansive attention on the other person that allows for the connection of two awarenesses at a deep and nonrational level of reciprocal relationship.

Attention, like everything else is vibration. Vibration, as well as attention, explains Borg, is relational. *Both healing and performance are based on the dance of vibratory interchange and connection.* Because attention is relational, the giver and receiver are participating in it together at all times, until there is no longer a giver or receiver but a mutual exchange of energies: healer and client, or in our case, the hearer and the heard. In the case of performance, we work with inclusive attention between actor and audience.

That attention is relational means that you've got responsiveness on both sides of that relationship. *Attention includes response. When you pay clear attention to something, it will begin to pay more attention to itself—and shift in a way that is healing to it, doing what it needs to do.* The attention is an "isness" that's already there between self and other, or self and other part of self, that you're turning your attention to[3] (italics mine).

This sensuous, sensitive communication is at the core of both healing and theatre. The listener is not by any means passive or static, but a partner in a dance, and one of our jobs is to keep the dance floor cleared and swept.

The following sequence of exercises requires a partner, the same one for the whole series.

A LONG SET OF EXERCISES IN LISTENING

1.

- Sit in straight-backed chairs facing each other. Decide who's Partner A and Partner B.
- Center and ground.
- Partner A: Put a hand gently on the lower thigh (near the knee) of your partner. Imagine yourself opening the lens of your attention so that your perception widens; let your attention *include* the other person within its parameters. (Please note the difference between "include" and "invade.")
- Keep breathing. Gradually begin to feel what, in the other person's subtle energy, moves within your perceptive frame. You may feel energy moving beneath your hand on the thigh. Notice it, follow it, do not try to *do* anything to or with it—simply *connect* to it and focus on its qualities and its mode of shifting, if there are indeed any shifts.
- Switch partners and repeat the exercise.
- Discuss what you each perceived.

2.

- Again, with the same partner, breathe, center and ground.
- Continue facing your partner, seated: Simultaneously, each of you gently places your right hand on the other's heart. Put your left hand on the hand of your partner, which is on your own heart. *Listen* with your *hands*. Open your attention to include both of you. What do you feel? See if you can feel a cycle of energy running through and between hearts, flowing through your arms and

---

[3]Borg, Susan Gallagher. Resonant Kinesiology Training Program.

hands, connecting the two of you. See if you can note in which direction the energy is running.

Let your hands down slowly. Breathe.

3.

Here is the actors' old tried and true mirror exercise done the same way, but with a shift in the nature of attention.

- Stand facing your partner. Center and ground.
- Begin by breathing. As Partner A breathes in, Partner B breathes out. Continue with this cycle of breaths for a few moments, as if you're sharing one circular stream of breath.
- Imagine that your energy field is expanding to include your partner—not with a pull or a yank or a suffocating heave—just gently opening your field enough so that your partner is standing within it.
- Partner A begins leading the movements: slowly moving hands, arms, torso, and/or legs at a pace Partner B can follow smoothly. No sharp turns, sudden shifts, or big surprises. The point is to create a mutual flow of movement. See if you can come to a point where, with no strain in following, it feels as if your bodies are connected by invisible threads. In fact, if you're in sync, invisible threads of connective energy actually begin to form between you.
- After a few moments, Partner B begins the leading. Include movement where the arms can relax a little; strain interferes with the connection and flow.
- See if you can come to a point where there's no leader or follower; you are simply swimming in synchronicity within the shared energy field you've developed. What does this feel like?
- Let the dance grow more intricate. See if the inclusive attention of both of you can deepen to take in a wider and more unexpected range of movement.
- When you're ready, let it go, shake it out, and take a few breaths. But keep your fields expanded if you can to include the other.

4.

- Both partners think of a common stance of their own, either seated or standing. Partner A, move into your stance: include posture, body alignment, position of hands, legs and feet, tilt of neck and head, where you're tense or relaxed, direction of the gaze of your eyes, what's going on in your face. Stay in this familiar stance, and after a moment, begin humming a favorite tune, or singing a favorite song with sounds but not actual words.

[Note: The stance does not have to be graceful or beautiful, and you don't have to be able to carry a tune! Just do what you do.]

- Partner B, watch and listen with your whole body-field. Move into that stance as if it is one of your own. Feel it in your bones, your blood-flow, your subtle energies. When you feel you're into it, start humming or singing with Partner A, who is still in the stance.
- After a moment or two, breathe it out, and switch roles.
- Breathe it out. Relax.

5.

- Find a place to sit with your partner where there's no one else too close: it's important to be where you don't have to whisper or mute the speaking in any way.
- Partner A, the storyteller: Take three to five minutes to tell of a time or event that changed your life. It might be a birth, a death, a divorce—but it also might be the time you had your first ice cream cone or when you saw a butterfly emerge from a cocoon. It does not, in other words, have to be earth-shattering drama—just a truthful and pivotal event that in some fashion changed you and that can be told in this circumscribed time limit.
- Partner B, the listener: Breathe, center and ground. Set your intention to listen wholly. Open your attention to include your partner. Expand your subtle body. Notice where in your partner you sense brightness or strength of energy. Notice (with your field even more than your mind) what kind of "music" comes through the way your partner speaks. What poetry or metaphor infuses the words? What's the nature and rhythm of silences or repetitions? What part(s) of the physical body is the voice resonating from: head? chest? belly? thighs? top of head? This does not have to be literal—just take in what it feels like to you. Notice the eyes of your partner as he speaks; what qualities of being do they reflect?
- Given both the content of the story and the manner of its being told, what chakras do you sense are most open? What levels of the field? How do you sense these things? As you listen, take the story into your own field wherever it rests in you, as if you yourself will be telling this same story in the first person, which in fact very shortly you will.

- The words are important, of course. They are of the essence. But they're not the whole story. The story lives within and around the person herself, in her body, and most certainly in her field. Be honest with yourself. You may be gripped, you may be bored, you may be anything in between. Listen for the breath of the story itself. Note as you open your attention to include the story what energies, what manner of life, is meeting you here.
- Do not interrupt: "Oh, I know just what you mean, Hilda! Last time that happened to *me* was when I was in the fourth grade when I..." Restrain yourself! Just listen. And when Partner A is finished, do not say, "Thank you for sharing," or you will go directly to jail without collecting $200.
- Take a moment of quiet for closure. Then switch roles.

6.

- Now you will tell each other's stories *in the first person,* as if it is *your* story. If you are doing this exercise in a class, you can tell the story (which has been heard only by you) to the whole group.
- Don't panic! Do *not* think you have to have it word for word. You've heard it only once; you've not taped or memorized it. You will of course leave things out or get them out of order, so forgive each other in advance for that. But if, because of how deeply you listened, you have perceived particular energy emphases of your partner as he or she spoke—chakras or levels of the field most open or vibrant—imagine your own field taking on that configuration.

  Along with the words and literal content you remember, along with body posture and vocal resonance and rhythms, move into the subtle energy strengths, the music, the beat of it. See if in the telling you can give a *whiff of the spirit* inside the story, its song. And if you can, what are you doing in relation to your own subtle body to reveal it?

  You need not try for everything! If you take on and move into just one or two qualities, it is enough.
- Next, Partner A tell Partner B's story, again in the first person, as above.

THE VOICE WITHIN THE VOICES

We each have many voices that we use in different situations, moods, or states of being. Somewhere within them is a voice that has a spark in it, a voice connecting to and reflecting something bigger than itself, a voice that knows instinctively how to bless, for it is blessed. I used to call it our "true voice," but that implies that all the others are false, which isn't so. They're just not all connected to our mysterious core, which seems forever singing the mystery out of which we come. That voice in us through which we speak closest to the bone is by no means a reflection of one's whole story; all our voices express in one way or another the diverse threads of experience and being. But there is something of courage, wisdom, and fierce love which appears to live uninhibited and unashamed inside that sparked voice. For a hundred and one reasons we mask it most of the time, mostly by forgetting, or fearing, that it's there.

In the case of spoken voice, truth is not necessarily beauty nor beauty truth, at least not to the ear. A fake voice can sound rich and mellifluous; the one with holy sparks in it might touch the ear haltingly or harshly. What is beautiful about a voice is not always its literal tone (though sometimes that's so too) but the quality of passion, blessing, and integrity it carries. No matter what its tone, pitch, vocabulary, or music, it bears a fundamental dignity.

We listen for all the voices, which are sometimes braided together. If our listening is hospitable enough, the "sparked voice" might walk into our "house" and settle in. But be careful how you seek to hear it; sometimes it's communicated through ways other than talking.

I know a woman who's a musician and massage therapist, whose grating, nasal voice and way of repeating everything make you want to run from the room. But when she plays the piano or is massaging the knots out of your muscles, her hands are speaking a voice from her core with a clarity, poignancy, and power she could not achieve through speech. I know a painter who staggers tediously through conversation like a drunkard, but whose paintings' brilliant eloquence speak the magic of the natural world in ways my words will never be able to do.

The sparked voice, in other words, is not always verbal, not even always vocal. Sometimes when it's being expressed through other means, the vocal-verbal expressions do sink into a mysterious music and poetry, but this isn't always the case, nor need it be.

The voice of a ninety-six-year-old Palestinian refugee I met in Syria was a cross between a handsaw and a raspy little bird. In the context of the whole of her, it made you want to clap your hands and dance. She spoke the grief of her exile, losses, years of wandering, yearning for home, and the scars of old wars; but she held her grief gently, almost gaily in the palm of her heart. "In the end of all," she chirped, "you must dance. You must sing! People come with their prune faces. They expect me to be sad about this life we've had. I have no time for them! You must make your blood light!" Her eyes twinkled, her tiny old arms danced and swayed. She became a little bird (how suitable the voice) flying through the branches of life's losses without ever getting tangled in them.

And of course there are some people graced with a natural beauty of tone and language who have nothing much to say. Gorgeous voices, completely disconnected from wisdom, soul, or truth, aren't everything.

Great pain or trauma within a person's story (or great joy and love, for that matter) can inform elements of true voice for the rest of one's life. You watch and listen for the voice in the face, the voice in the movements. In Cambodia the stories of some people lived in their eyes. All the adults I interviewed had been to hell and back. Some, according to the voice in their eyes, still weren't *back*. The flood of their words was countered by a closed, impenetrable gaze—guarded, veiled, frozen in sorrow, or hardened into a look of perpetual shock like a deer before bright headlights. Other Cambodian eyes were rich with uncommon and mysterious wisdom, drawing others backward into times and places that would forever be unknown and incomprehensible to us. Those eyes shone with more than physical survival, but with the light of what it takes a human spirit to come through the worst still breathing, a kind of transcendent mixture of grief and endurance that words alone could not have captured.

There will be times when the hardness or even ugliness of a masked voice is indeed so much of who that person has become that the truer, deeper voice may no longer be available to be heard. Just note it. Who knows what happened—to them or to their forebears—who knows what closed a voice's conduit to heart and soul.

Sparked voice and all the other voices in whatever way they are expressed are themselves part of the story: speaking of what's hidden and what's revealed, what's too hot to touch and what can be held firmly, what's true and what's confused. While never ignoring the other voices, what we listen for as a possible thread underneath—through the words and all that's beyond the words—is the voice of the soul in its manifold guises, the voice of the song in the story.

HINTS AND CLUES ABOUT INTERVIEWING

Listening includes the right kind of questions. If you sit down with someone, whip out your tape recorder, and say, "Okay, so what's your story?" chances are what you'll get will be vague and confused.

First, always explain to people why you're interviewing them; not to do so is the height of disrespect and exploitation. Ask them if, for the sake of your dramatic work, an interview is okay. Sometimes it's not. Let it be. Before you ask any questions aloud, you need to know the real unspoken questions inside your heart and why you're here to begin with, implying that you're ignorant of something or you wouldn't be on this quest. Why have you come to this person, this place, this group, this culture, at this time? What do you wish to understand? In giving them an idea of where you're coming from, you're offering a bit of your own story and making a place where your two stories can meet. If you have your answers in advance, go home.

In Bosnia, for example, my underlying question was not, "What happened to you in the war?" which is a journalist's kind of question, but "How do human beings survive such suffering and loss? What is it in us and around us that moves toward healing? What is it that fails to heal? How do people move on with their lives after a catastrophe that has changed the very nature of what they knew as home?" You may never speak these initial questions to your interviewees, but that's where you're starting from. And whatever your questions, there needs to be a sincere craving to know and understand, whether or not there can ever be a clear answer that wraps it all up nicely in a tight little bundle.

Before you travel to a foreign place, of course, research its history and current situation so that your interviews have an informed context.

I've had people say, "My story? Impossible!" Your questions then become very simple and direct. The following dialogue is from an interview with an Israeli woman who began, "I don't have a story! I have a life! Go ask Sarah or Chava, *they* have stories. I wouldn't know where to begin!"

"Well, where were you born?"

"In Bulgaria."

"Ah, and when was that?"

"Well, all right. I'm no spring chicken. I was born in 1929."

"Oh, so you were a child in Bulgaria during the Holocaust?"

"Ya, well *that's* a story." (She tells it, with crackling bluntness.)

"So after the war, didn't the Communists come to Bulgaria?"

"Oh my God, *that's* a story." (She tells it.)

"How did you and your family get to Israel?"

"You don't know what Ben Gurion did to get us over? I'll tell you..."

(She does.)

"And so you started life over in Israel?"

"Oh my God, from scratch. You know what that was like? Let me tell you ..." (She does.)

Three hours later, story upon story upon story, her "I don't have a story" has come to life. Your job is to open small door after small window, a nudge here, a prod there, and after a while, a tall complex story made of shorter ones walks in and takes up the whole room. With both the larger, unspoken questions in your heart (the framework of the "house") and the smaller spoken questions of the interview (doors and windows), you are holding the ground and defining the quality of the space the story is entering.

Knowing *when* to ask for stories and when to be patient and take in other kinds of communication is important as well. I interviewed a Palestinian woman in a farming village in the hills of the West Bank. It was during the first *intifadah* in the late 1980s; things were very tense. I was the first Jew Fatimah had ever met other than the soldiers who had cut off her water and electricity, ransacked her home, slapped her to the ground, and imprisoned her son. So here I come with my little tape recorder and my translator (a young Palestinian man from the city), and I'm expecting this woman to open up to me? Not likely. At first she was polite but formal and brittle. She began telling her story in brief fragments, nervous and ill at ease, looking out the glassless windows to see if she was being watched, jumping up repeatedly to bring more Coke in little tea glasses. We went walking in the hills, and she told me the story of the land. We visited a neighbor who was sewing the extraordinarily beautiful Palestinian embroidery. I asked to see Fatimah's embroidery. Pleased, she gave me one of her long, embroidered dresses to wear for the day. We started laughing. We looked like sisters. I asked her how her outdoor oven worked. She showed me how they bake their bread, and sitting on the ground we ate a lunch of fragrant flatbread dribbled with oil and rosemary. Hours later, when I asked again about her imprisoned son, she wept and began speaking her personal story from the desire to do so. Tears and laughter flowed easily. She poked me in the ribs to make a point. When I left, we embraced.

I didn't go knowing that this is how it would need to be. I went with five more appointments for interviews afterward, all of which were missed. I went stupidly and brazenly in those days, thinking that a story comes when one asks for it, not when it is good and ready. Fatimah was one of many from whom I learned certain lessons about respect, not as a mental abstraction, but as a way of patience, a way of honest curiosity and presence, a way of respecting that a story has its own body, heart, and spirit and will not be forced against its will into the open.

On my first of two trips to Bosnia, the war had been over for less than a year. The trip was not about, "Oh hello. I'm a playwright whose work reflects women surviving disastrous circumstances. I know you have just suffered terribly. May I exploit your pain and write about your lives? Great. So, what happened to *you*?" Even if I'd been that cheap, the still traumatized women were in no condition to speak about what had happened to them in more than incoherent fragments. On that first trip I asked nothing. Stories did indeed come to me from all corners throughout the journey, but I did not ask anyone to "be interviewed." In general, too, it's not wise to go grab a people's stories and give nothing back. Story is gold. You consider what you can exchange for such treasure. In that case, I was there teaching the basics of hands-on healing in daily workshops. After a year, I returned. This time, the women knew and trusted me and had become aware of the fact that many in the United States know very little about the reality of their lives before or during the war, and nothing of how human beings move on afterward with the hell of it by no means over, just quieter and less sensational. This time they *wanted* to speak their tales, both individually and in groups, the need to speak coming from their own hearts and wills, not just my desire to understand, and this too changed the nature of how the stories were offered.

Understanding the larger tapestry of who they were included their singing the folk songs they'd grown up with, bringing in their needlework (laces, embroideries, knitted sweaters, crocheted coats), and cooking a feast of their best dishes. When I discovered that some were planning to miss the feast because they lacked the money to buy the ingredients, I gave them each a stipend, calling it "business expenses" as part of my "research" into the living culture of Bosnia.[4] They pocketed

---

[4]Where, you might ask, does all that money come from to fund such trips and pay for translators, and give out stipends, and cover all the many expenses involved in such story-gathering. Most of us have no golden egg in our bank accounts, and the money is not easy to come by. But it's always possible. The three ways I've used most are grant-writing, benefit performances, and asking donations from people I know (trip contributions make great birthday and Christmas presents).

their fistfuls of money, and we had a feast to end all feasts, each woman photographed as she held up her favorite dish, each tasting everyone else's and throwing out compliments like confetti, each wrapping bits of their food in bags or foil for me to "take home to my American friends, so they should taste our lives." And then they danced, weaving a stomping, clapping, circle dance round and round the overloaded tables, celebrating even as they wept.

Stories, in sum, wherever you go and in whatever manner you fill yourself with them, are not just about words spoken into your tape recorder. They're in the flying fingers that make such delicate lace, in the precise spicing of the meatballs, in the expert folding of a giant piece of flatbread fresh from the walls of a mud oven, in the guarded eyes of a survivor, in the high-kicking steps of a grief-streaked dance. And both the tears and the laughter pour forth more freely with the gradual comprehension that one's story is *worth* being heard, that it is something of great *value* to the world.

> True art evolves us—opens our arms and weakens our prejudices so that the ever-present seeds of healing and renewal can take root in our soul and sinew, and cause joy.[5]

At the heart of any monologue we perform will be the heart with which we listened to the world and let its stories crack us open. In the end, if what is taken in through our ears, intellect, eyes, body, and even our subtle energies has not filtered in a stream straight through the heart and been quickened by its pulse, then nothing has been heard for what it is. The actual, unabashed love of human beings and the relief and wonder in the face of both our differences and commonality (including both the thrill and the joy of us, as well as the grief and the disgust), our capacity to weep and rage for the ugliest and most damning of our ways with the same tears that flow for the brilliance and magnificence, is what in the end leads us to *hear*—a word that rests easy in the *heart*.

---

[5]Ladinsky, Daniel. 1999. *The Gift: Poems by Hafiz.* New York: Penguin. p. 3.

5

Transmuting Story into Monologue

IN THE BEGINNING, THERE WAS CHAOS

This part—transforming an ungainly mass of disorganized materials and information into an economical and elegantly expressive dramatic framework, and recasting disparate, intimate tales specific to a people, a time, a place into a broadly meaningful and cohesive work that illumines the hidden corners of our shared soul—is hard. Just plain hard. It is also what worthwhile theatre is about. Like all forms of artistic creation, it can be messy, frustrating, confusing, ego-denting, and take an inordinately long time. You begin to suspect it's impossible. You decide you were an idiot for taking it on. You consider a career in accounting. You may have to try thirteen ways of looking at your monologue before sorting out the right design, which is simply the way with crafting anything of beauty and value. Don't give up. Take time. Take heart.

Because a chapter on this topic should by no means be a chapter but a book, please accept what's here as an *introduction*, framed not as a how-to manual, but as a compass to chart your direction. Every monologue's design is fashioned from a unique set of materials, history, dreams, questions, and possibilities, and there is no one formula for untangling, cutting, and tying together the long dangling threads of a bunch of stories into a finely knotted drama (a blessing, actually, as God forbid we should bore ourselves to death with doing the same thing over and over). So you'll find no one-size-fits-all exercises in this section, just examples, suggestions, hints, and clues toward shaping your monologue with an eye to three things:

- its *Heart* (content),
- its *Bone* (structure),
- and—tacked shamefully into a corner at the end, another topic worthy of a book—its *Words*.

The examples offered in this and the next chapter on character are from my own monologues, a fact that makes my teeth itch with embarrassment at how arrogant the choices may appear. Please forgive and bear with me. I use these examples not because I think they're brilliant or the best or the only, but simply because I know the process of their transformation from inchoate materials into the dramatic form they became, which is the concern of these two chapters.

HEART (CONTENT)

1. *Relighting the Spark*

Though there are many possibilities of getting started, often you'll find yourself sitting on a mountain of disordered, fractured bits and pieces of material collected, observed, and imagined, knowing that you must somehow make sense, form, and contained beauty of it all, wishing the fragments would either self-edit and self-assemble or blow up. Before you light a match to it in frustration, go back to the spark that initially fired you (see Chapter 1) and put your match to that spark. Reignite it. Remember why you began. What was the passion, the quest, the dream, the ache in the heart, the puzzle? What was the "first step of your journey of a thousand miles" setting you in the specific direction you chose?

Whatever the nature of that spark, keep it as a small torch by your materials as you reexamine them to light the words, images, sounds, and ideas while you ponder their nature and content and look for what connects them at the core. If you have not held interviews but have assembled other kinds of notes, go through them with the same eye for detail, nuance, and suggestiveness in what you've gathered, holding up that same torch, ever open for continual surprise and discovery. It is *you* who—through your questions, generosity of heart, and intelligent capacity for wonder—must perceive and illumine the extraordinary in the ordinary, the exquisite taste of hard-earned joy, the elegance of honest grief, the mystery of our lives at that core.

2. *When basing your monologue on real people*...

If you've held interviews and have a pile of audio tapes, start by transcribing them yourself. "What? Are you kidding? It'll take ten years. Completely inefficient. Get me a professional typist!" As a friend of mine says, "Efficiency is highly overrated." Transcribing is, yes, a long, painstaking process, but well worth the time. Listening to those voices again so slowly, phrase-by-phrase, as you type, you're drawn back to the place, the smells, the slant of light, the taste of the food, the pull of your heart one way or another, the sounds, the quality of the air, and of course most important, to the people themselves, individually and together. You hear again, coming back to you fresh and aromatic, thoughts, feelings, words, and phrases you may have forgotten or not heard for what they were. You're reminded as well of the subtle qualities of each human being, her field, her music, this once-only style of presence on the earth. And knowing that some of these people may find their way in one form or another into a dramatic character, you listen with your own whole body-field, for the meaning of the words themselves certainly, but also and significantly for the tones, the accents, the vibrations, the rhythms, the silences, the resonance of sound inside the body.

Get everything down in the transcribing, even repetitions, stumblings, and pauses. The goal here is not to end up with archives of oral history, but the details will be helpful in finding the underlying essence; the details *create* the essence, and the essence the details. And even if your monologue ends up entirely fictional with imagined characters and original text, it's worth the time of transcribing your tapes as faithfully as you can. You never know what thin thread will filter into the final characters and content, however subtly or slantwise, to grant it the taste it needs. (Think how small, how fine—how costly!— is a small bit of saffron, and how three teeny-tiny threads in a dish can change its whole nature.)

The heart at the center of the body of your monologue, nourishing the whole, will not always come directly from your interviews or the people themselves. Always there are stories within stories within stories. Another way of saying it is that there are stories that surround and embrace the ones you will hear.

It's important to know about a place, its history, its culture—whether it's 1940s Berlin, 1970s Chile, last year on a peninsula in the Sea of Okhotsk, or yesterday on the Upper West Side of Manhattan. Where relevant, know and take in its music, the art, the literature, the folk tales, the customs strange or familiar. Wash yourself in the sound of its language, its song.

Consider the stories *about* your gathering of the stories—the experiences of this journey from inception to end, the adventures, impressions, surprises, obstacles, observations, new understandings, and study of that place and its people (which "place and people" might again be two blocks away, at the farm over the hill, or halfway around the world). What have you gleaned of its situation? How do you perceive its relation to we who may be very different and in different circumstances? All these ingredients are thrown into the pot; they might turn out the base stock of the soup.

It's interesting too that individuals living day-to-day inside a trying and difficult situation may have no perspective about their own peculiar qualities of spirit, will, or resilience that sustain them through hard times. But we, looking in from the outside, can acquire that insight (a person's or people's innate sense of humor, for example, or dedication to education for their children, or level-headed patience in the face of endless obstacles). It goes into the pot. Much that you witness and experience will not be reflected in the words of the interviews, yet may turn out to be a significant nutrient in your monologue's blood cells.

On my first trip to post-war Bosnia, I brought gifts and letters from my women friends at home to the struggling women there. On the first day, as the first of the letters was read, the Bosnians began quietly to weep. "Sisters!" they whispered. "We have sisters. We didn't know you knew or thought about us." In the solo play which evolved from those trips, the main character, Minka, speaks through both acts to an audience she can neither see nor hear, but she persists in addressing the possibility of its attentive existence from the need to believe that there's a world out there who listens and cares.

MINKA (*to audience*)

When I imagine you, I think there had to be one moment for you, just one moment, da?—when all here was at its worst, and you saw our faces and heard our cries, and you stopped what you were doing to look, to listen. At that one moment you perhaps stopped your car, or put down your book, looked up from your computer screen, or told the children to wait a minute before their dessert. Or you sat down or stood up, or moved closer, or took a step back. Or maybe you stopped stirring the soup, or scrubbing, or singing, or you straightened your back from weeding the garden, or said to your friend, "I have to get off now. I'll call you later." Just for that one moment—I believe it— you stopped.

Everybody says, "No, they didn't. No one stopped anything. They went on with their lives, Minka, don't be absurd. They are very busy persons, you've become such a fool!" But I've never been interested in what Everybody has to say. They're always wrong, this Everybody. I know them. And what they do not say is, "We never stopped. We never looked. We never listened. That is how we come out so smart about such things!" Da. That part they leave out. Don't bother with them.

No, I like to think that for that one moment of stillness, you saw half a mil-lion looks of misery and heard the screams and weeping, and you caught your breath. And maybe—I don't know this for sure, but maybe—a few of you wept.

Whoever you are, wherever you are—thank you.

But if you are there, if indeed you do exist, please—what it is I wish to say to you is this.

That there was something before that moment when you stopped to look or listen. We breathed before that. We had a life, a history, a soup of all the ingredients it takes to make a little world. I also have this fear, you see, for-give me please if I am wrong, that when you watched this sea of grieving faces, and heard the sounds of anguish and of fear, you thought, "Yes, look at them. That is who they are. That is who they always were, those people from far places. That is who they were born to be, another wagonload of vic-tims."

And I want to shake my fist at you, you Everybodies! Please. Understand it. There Was a Before. It was round and fat, and we were marvelous and stu-pid and brave and cowardly—we were Alive! Before. And there were losses before. There were some dreams that died, and we spilled coffee on our new white blouses and twisted ankles on the ice. We made mistakes, told dirty sto-ries, liked good food, got sometimes drunk. We loved, we hated, we sang, we danced. Do you understand?

We didn't then look all the same as we look now, or as perhaps you see us. We didn't trudge along the roads together with carts and blankets, weeping, in numbers no one can count. We were Not born for this!

Or if we were—then so were you.
Do you understand?[1]

Though nothing in or related to that speech was ever spoken to me by the Bosnian women, it was inscribed in their reality, and given the nature of our craft where footnotes don't apply, we have the luxury of telling the story in ways that flesh out its contours. Our work, though it may be based on or inspired by actual tales and events, is never itself fact. Even when we fashion a character entirely on a real person, even when we use eighty-five percent of the words as told to us, still it is not fact. It is life filtered, swirled, shaped, and articulated through our own dramatic imaginations, and we are *always* taking poetic license, which is one of the very tools of our work. We may have begun with fact; but we hope to end with truth.

So you read again (and again) all that you have transcribed or written down. You make notes of events, insights, and observations of your *own* story on this journey that are part of the overall picture. And then you look for lights, shadows, and connections. You highlight those passages, stories, or pieces of stories, ideas, phrases, and moments that make you weep, make you laugh, fill you with wonder, help you understand, cause you to tear your hair out, or make you glad to be alive. Those things that remind you again, or teach you for the first time, what the whole piece is about in relation to the human soul, and how these stories *connect:* connect to each other, connect to the throbbing world, connect to our learning how on earth to live our lives, connect to our wishing to grasp what it means to be human, what it means to be part of all life. Such highlighted passages do not have to be answers to your initial questions so much as reflections of them. They do not have to be snippets of sharp intellectual brilliance, or be eloquently worded (although sometimes they are both; the amount of poetry that can pour through the raw notes is astonishing). They are simply glowing coals, unearthed clues, usable shards of beauty, pain, and insight. There is no order to them yet. You don't know how or where in the piece they'll be used. But as you wade through and weed out what you will leave behind, what remains are like little iron filaments sliding toward a magnet of meaning at the center.

---

[1]Lubar, Deborah. 2000. *Naming the Days.* pp. 8–10.

And hopefully, because it's a good thing, a necessary thing, a crucial thing, inside that magnetic core is a hot and heavy dose of paradox and irony. For the thing is, although the shape of your monologue needs to be coherent and well-designed, its beginning, middle, and ending lucid and understandable, the stories it holds—if they really have to do with the human soul—will not usually have such smooth cohesion or fitted hinges at the corners. They, in contrast to the drama's design, will be bumpy and irregular, laced with contrasting truths and diverse perspectives, and it's a good bet there won't be a sigh-of-relief denouement where all the pieces come happily together at the end and everything is tidily resolved. On the contrary, while the monologue must be resolved *dramatically,* the stories we're after will end with a beginning, or on the notes of an unresolved suspension. Hope for a bittersweet tension between the needed closure of the monologue itself and the lack of closure in its story. For if you want your story to "sing the most beautiful song in the world" that its sound splinter our hearts in just the right place, then the heart of the story itself needs to be made of a wedding of light and shadow, laughter and tears, joy and anguish, a heart strong and vital enough to hold that rough rubbing together of opposing forces which we grapple with all our lives.

There may be times you research or collect stories from a place, person, or people where the overarching or immediate situation is so horrendous you wonder how to create a drama true to these stories that isn't two tons of relentless grimness. How to infuse tales of difficulty, struggle, and suffering with hope, redemption, and even humor, which may not come through in the stories as told or discovered? For you never ever, ever want to bury an audience in unmitigated, unleavened misery. We can get it for free by turning on the news, every single day. But how to create such leaven without dishonesty, superficial idealism, or cheap sentimentality?

It's not easy. It may take a lot of time to sort it out with integrity. But it distinguishes theatre from some other forms of truth telling. It's the painting of the picture with a greater palette of color and range of texture concerning our human condition than may come through elsewhere. As noted before, one thing we're starved for these days is the sheer *acknowledgement* of the complexities and ironies of our lives, and for their being offered to us in ways so magnificent, even when they're ugly or harsh, that we move to embrace rather than flee them.

The starting point is your own compassion and respect for the whole truth of the situation and your fearlessness in the face of what that truth holds. The luminousness and even love with which you bear witness will filter through your story and into your characters' thoughts, hearts, words, and ways. Often the warm blood of a fully etched character as she tells a tough story can be what melts the edges of the icy circumstances. And even in the most horrendous moments of a narrative, a character can maintain her sense of humor, which runs like veins of gold through tales of grief. Rough humor, bizarre humor, sweet and sour humor, wry or ridiculous humor. It is, in other words, the nature and complexity of the hearts of the *people who inhabit* the story that work upon the quality of the story's own heartbeat. And all of it is influenced, always, by the intelligence and fiber of your own heart, one more thing that can't be faked.

On any quest for the truth of us, we do well to relax our grip on the search for scrubbed and neatly packaged summations of our nature, as whatever Lady Truth may be, she isn't going to show up unrumpled and sweet-smelling. You never know about Truth. You might catch a glimpse of her tail as she slides away through tall grasses, or a whiff of her musk, a scratch of her howl, then her purr. She—just like our own souls—is not what we would have her be, unstained, unruffled, well-behaved, and itemized. Expect the unguessed and unforeseen, the improbable and unbargained-for. It's something to keep in mind as you climb the mountain of your stories or rummage around in the attics and basements of your experiences, notes, and observations in search of the heart of your characters and the heartbeat of your monologue. Lady Truth does not just *hold* more than one story at a time, she *is* more than one story at a time

3. Monologue of Imagined People

Barring the transcribing of interviews, it's much the same as above, for imagined characters as well as their stories must also be *true, real,* and *coherent* with blood that flows and hearts that beat. The seed usually arises from observations and experiences of real people and from our same driving questions. Our work then, as with all writers, is to fashion of the disparate elements of truth, fantasy, and questions a story that walks honestly on the soil of our earth with real legs.

Sometimes we breathe new life into old, familiar stories. In a monologue called "Eve's Version," an aging, matronly Eve tells the story of what really transpired in Eden, fleshing out the bare bones of the tale we know by heart, remembering the frustrations and puzzlements of her growing consciousness, the ups and downs of her arranged marriage to Adam, and learning from her beloved teacher—a giant water serpent named Grandmother Snake—to hear the many sounds of God's voice beyond the punishing one from above. She tells a story of longing and loss, betrayal and forgiveness, and the willingness to risk change. When at last she bites into the apple, she tells us

At that moment, all the world changed. This apple of blood red, it tasted both of sweet and of sour. Both of beauty and of pain. All in the same bite! You have to understand that everything in Eden was sweet, and we thought everything outside must be bitter or sour. But here they were together in the flesh of this one fruit, and the taste of it, the taste of it broke my heart into a thousand pieces, and some of them went scattering on the ground like seeds. And I was filled up to bursting. The fire inside me was rising so fast, I thought that I might split in two from the tension of this sweet and bitter fruit.[2]

All our stories—real, imagined, or from the vast territory in between—are a bite into that apple. A filling up to bursting from that sweet and bitter food.

BONE (STRUCTURE)

I've found it shocks many young writer-performers that monologue has to be held up by a dramatic structure at all. Why can't you get up there and blather fascinatingly for an hour and a half and go home? Some say you can. It's true that the structure of monologue is more malleable and subtle than that of traditional dramas where you have stricter demands of plot and character conflict; but with a solo piece you still have to answer (to varying degrees and often in a more muted fashion) many of the same old questions about dramatic architecture.

If you are writing a piece about your own life and speaking as yourself, á la Spalding Gray, the design of the story's weave may be looser, but it's still there. For the kind of monologue this book suggests—those involving characters and complex situations of people and places quite different from your cultural milieu—the need for a clear and cogent framework is heightened, and it's that kind of frame on which this

---

[2]Lubar, Deborah. 1997. *Eve's Version*. p. 19.

chapter focuses. For monologue about your own story, please turn to the other fine books out now on creating monologue.

There are indeed those blessed times when you know right from the outset the form you wish your monologue to take. (As Rosalind says in *As You Like It*, "Get down on your knees and thank God, fasting," for such good fortune; who knows when it will happen again.) And all writers and actors know there are times when you're nudged forward toward the right shape by strange, serendipitous, even ridiculous events. Like the time I'd prepared for a storytelling festival some new versions of old tales about the Baal Shem Tov, the mystical Jewish Hasidic leader of two centuries ago. After working on them for some time, I practiced telling them for the festival's producer, who fell asleep about halfway through. This didn't bode well. I worked to reframe the stories, retold them again a week or so later, and was mortified as her eyes once more grew heavy and her head began to nod.

At that time, my mother happened to send me a pair of lavender shoes with pointy toes and big square rhinestones that she'd found in some bargain basement for $2.99. "Just your color!" she wrote. "Don't you love them?" If I lived to be a hundred and five I would never have bought those shoes. But when I put them on, they made me have to slather my face with eye shadow, lipstick, and rouge, put my hair in curlers, and begin operating like my grandmothers' friends from another era. I went down to the consignment shop and took back the bulky seal-skin jacket I'd left there a year before (another gift from Mom). I put on the shoes and the jacket, added jewels and a flowered hat, made up my face like the old Yiddish ladies from downtown New York, spent three months getting drenched in the history and literature of the old East European *shtetls*, and somewhere between the reading and the outfit, the peppery and opinionated character of Rose Solomon was conjured into being who, in her heavy Yiddish accent, wove her own outrageous tellings of the Hasidic stories into the tale of her childhood in the Old World. Rose told those tales a thousand times better than I could. Furthermore, she had the chutzpah to yell at her audience not to fall asleep at the mention of the Baal Shem Tov: "I don't care how you do it—punch each other, pinch yourselves, take a diet pill, do *anything*—but stay awake!"

The one-act monologue, "Rose Solomon and The Baal Shem Tov," born from the failure to tell some stories in my own voice, plus an unexpected gift of ill-chosen shoes, ended on the eve of Rose's departure from Poland for the New World and toured for a year. Audiences would ask, "So what happens to her on the Lower East Side?" Who knew? Thus, Act II: "Luigina Ponzini and the Song of the Madonna," which required research into the plight of four million starving southern Italians who fled to *La Merica* at the turn of the century, and in which Rose's story is continued through the mouth of her friend "Crazy Luigina," a Catholic peasant who meets Rose on the boat over and becomes her sister in spirit through lives of hardship and heartbreak in the New World. Twelve years later, the two-act monologue is still running.

This is a long-winded way of saying that you don't always have methodical, well-plotted plans to get a piece going; the universe with its inimitable sense of humor occasionally drops shining bizarrely shaped pebbles on your path, and your job is to see them for what they are and follow where they lead.

Sometimes your structure will be as simple as a series of brief monologues loosely strung together, each a different character (as in the monologues of the brilliant character actor Danny Hoch). Or you know from the outset that your setting is an immigration center and you want seven immigrants there with stories to tell as they're being processed. Or you will have one set prop on a stage, as in the monologue "The Syringa Tree" by Pamela Gien, for which a swing was used as a fulcrum for the character to tell her story of growing up in South Africa under Apartheid, the important people in her childhood (all played by her) passing through the tale. In such cases, the piece's design is clean, spare, and direct. No problem.

But other times, you will need something unique to the issues or the characters at hand, a more complex skeleton to support and express them.

First, if you've gathered your stories from real people, consider *how closely you will adhere to the original stories and people.* For example:

- You will almost always have to delete, add, and rearrange; a story as told to someone rarely has an inherently economical or dramatic shape. But still you may wish to stay faithful to sections of the original wording. Will you be true to some stories and fictionalize others? Will you fictionalize the whole piece?
- Will you use one long story for the whole text? Or a multiplicity of shorter stories, creating of them a dramatic construct within which they speak to and enhance one another?

- How many characters are needed to tell the stories? One? Four? Thirty, none of them probed very deeply, each with only a brief speech, but all of them together creating the multifaceted voice of a complex community—as Anna Deveare Smith has done in her one-woman shows? If more than one character, will they address one another? (It's possible, even though you're playing them all.) Or will they speak their tales without acknowledging one another's existence?
- Will a character be based wholly on one person you've met or come out as an amalgam of the qualities and stories of several real people? Or will a character, though inspired by the circumstances of actual people, be a totally imagined creation with a personality and words of her own?

Next, remind yourself of the familiar questions underlying all dramatic frames.

1. *What* is this monologue about?
2. *Where* and *When* is this all taking place?
3. *Who* is telling the story or stories?
4. *What* are the given circumstances?
5. *To Whom* is the story being told?
6. *Why* does the character need to speak it?

The first four questions are approached as with any dramatic piece.

1. What is the monologue about?

It's about your questions with the sparks inside them. It's about what was discussed in the section on heart. One suggestion: Don't be too broad, as in, "It's about the human soul." "It's about good and evil." "It's about surviving incest." True, perhaps, but go further. What *aspect* of the human soul, and whose, and in relation to what? What *about* good and evil, and who cares? What *about* the survival of incest and with what perspective that touches on those of us who have not suffered it? To say a monologue is "about Bosnia" is only a start. To say it's "about how human beings in such a place (and there are many) manage their first small steps of healing after a devastating war has shattered their lives and homes" comes closer to the bone.

2. *Where and When*

You need to clarify and distinguish between (1) the time, place, and circumstances *of the story told* (i.e., a *shtetl* in Poland 100 years ago); and (2) the time, place, and circumstances *of the monologue through which the story is expressed right now* (i.e., on this stage, in this theatre, at this time, in front of this audience). For example, *the stories* are about the years of World War II in Germany; t*he setting of the monologue* is the living room of an apartment in Berlin, fifty years later.

3. *Who is telling this story?*

Assuming you're entering another persona, who exactly is (or are) your character(s)? The next chapter will sink more deeply into this topic; for now it's important to recognize that *how a dramatic story is shaped, offered, received, and understood, how it reveals its essence and meaning,* always *depends on who is telling it.*

In fact, the writing and structuring of your piece go hand in hand with the creation of character. Sometimes the whole idea for the monologue is propelled from the beginning by one compelling character, all other decisions arising from how to bring her to life on the stage, which means that on occasion, it's the personality of the *Who* that determines *what this piece is about.* Other times *what it's about* and how that content demands to be expressed helps you arrive at *who tells it.*

Whoever they are, you want characters who meet and match the complexity and the heart of the story: three-dimensional beings with an intrinsic weave of contrasting thoughts and behaviors—like actual humanity. Beware of any qualities that obscure the *complexity* of the soul we're claiming to probe, which requires moving beyond the current predilection in our culture for:

- predictable, prefabricated representations of human beings,
- characters defined only by one glaring, consistent quality (The Fearful one, The Angry One, The Cowardly One, The Brave One. . .),
- one-dimensional life-sized stand-ups who have passions and pursuits as thin as the cardboard they're made of, so self-absorbed they have no clue of the world's realities beyond their block, or
- characters whose dramatic purpose is to stand in for or represent an *idea* or *point of view* in contrast to the other characters' representative points of view (put them all together, they spell one human being).

Complex comes from the words *com:* "together," and *plexus:* "braided." In our work it's the braiding together of the many strands of a person's traits and potential rather than a highlighting of only one, expressing the force and intricacy not only of the person herself, but in part, the story she speaks and inhabits. In part, it is this braiding and rubbing together of the many-colored aspects of one's being that lead to our eccentric, peculiar, and outrageously *un*predictable human ways. (The characters in European films are usually spiced heavily with such luscious eccentricity if you're looking for some hints and clues.)

4. What are the given circumstances?

The given circumstances pertain to the monologue itself within which the stories rest. With Rose Solomon the given circumstances are simply that an old lady comes down to earth from the afterworld and blathers for an hour to this audience. Many monologues are as simply devised. In Danny Hoch's one-man shows, a series of characters unrelated to each other speak for a while about their lives. *We* do not always know exactly where they are or why they are speaking to us, but clearly *they* know and are at home both in that place and in the need to express themselves. Each character is well-grounded in the context of his or her world and has invited us into that place with integrity, three-dimensionality, and openness. It's enough.

Some pieces require a more cohesive and specific construct. In the fictional monologue I wrote inspired by Bosnian women, the *Who* are three women just returned to their country having been refugees elsewhere while the war raged, and now coping with their losses in entirely different ways. Not knowing the fate of their loved ones, they have returned to a broken shambles of what once was home and must literally and figuratively pick up the pieces of what's left and move forward. The set is a surreal wasteland of rags, broken housewares, and debris.

In sum: for monologue there will be times when the given circumstances equal a character on stage talking directly to an audience, and times when they're as complex as those of a traditional play.

The last two questions are especially important for monologue.

5. To Whom are the characters speaking?

More often than not it's the audience.

If there's more than one character, they can also address one another, although not in a conventional clipped back-and-forth dialogue of traditional drama, which is difficult for a solo performer to carry off without being tedious and looking foolish.

In Marianne Lust's two-act monologue *You Do What You Do*, about Countess Maria von Maltzan, a crusty, eccentric, German aristocrat who became a member of the anti-Hitler Resistance, the actor playing von Maltzan is onstage alone, but the aging Countess reminisces in the living room of her Berlin apartment surrounded by five (invisible) humans and three (invisible) animals whom she is constantly addressing and responding to but whom the audience never sees. It is within these conversations and because of these relationships that she tells of the war years and her escapades in the underground. In one short scene she is shifting her focus and her comments between four humans with conflicting agendas and one misbehaving dog. The audience, who is never acknowledged, observes through the fourth wall, and it is up to the solo actor to bring the invisible presences to blood-pumping life.

When the audience, however, *is* being addressed directly, the important thing is what that audience *signifies* to the characters: that is, *who specifically* the audience is in the character's mind and heart, and what relationship the character has or develops with them during the course of the piece.

6. Why does the character need to tell the story?

In monologue this question is the trickiest, sometimes the most subtle and contrived, and the most often ignored. Unlike a traditional drama with more than one character where the objectives, tensions, and struggles of each are clear and prominent, in monologue it can be a subterranean matter, sometimes with a mundane and overly obvious answer, but the question needs to be asked nonetheless. Your character must have some *need to be heard*, no matter how hidden, how briefly noted, how simplistic, how complex. The need helps shape the trajectory, even if that trajectory is simply the movement through a story from beginning to end. What the character actually *receives* from an audience is up for grabs—it depends on the nature of the piece, the character, and the motivation, but the need itself of the audience's attentiveness influences profoundly the manner in which the stories are offered, and often the design of the whole.

Even in personal monologues like Spalding Gray's, I always assumed from his manner that he was obsessed not only with the neurotic twists and turns of his own life in the context of our culture, but also with *sharing* his experiences and perceptions as well. It wasn't a highly dramatic reason or complicated or terribly intriguing in itself; but if it's a real and potent need, it's enough. It works.

The motivation might be more contrived and still simple. In *Rose Solomon and the Baal Shem Tov,* Rose mentions at the beginning of the piece that she's dead already so you might wonder what on earth she's doing here.

Ya, that's a good question. I don't know what I'm doing here. They con-tacted me up where I am now. They said, "Rose Solomon, Rose Solomon! Yoo-hoo! Rose!! Listen, Rose, the world is going through a lot of troubles now. We got problems, craziness you would not believe. Please, Rose, come back down here and tell us some stories to perk us up. . . . Someone from your time, your tribe, your place, you'll know from troubles, you'll have the right stories. . . ."

And so against her better instincts, Rose comes down, yaks her way through an hour of stories and finds she enjoys the spotlight, but ini-tially she's there just because *they* (whoever "they" are) asked her to come and cheer us up. It's enough.

On another level, the life, the heart, and the energy of those very real human beings seated in the theatre, the ones bearing witness to *your* bearing witness, are what keep a performer going in any monologue where you and that audience *are* the ensemble. So the actor as well as the character has a true need of their attentiveness.

AN EXAMPLE OF SETTING THE BONES

I offer here an illustration of transmuting the material to monologue, using the two-act piece *Blood & Stones* to sketch out how the six basic questions were answered, and how the nature of material and story gathering directly informed the design. It's an example of just one monologue, at one time, about one set of stories based on interviews, but hopefully it illumines a bit of the process.

When I went to Israel and the West Bank to understand how the his-torical conflict shared by Jew and Arab had informed the personal lives of ordinary women, I interviewed women of many backgrounds, per-sonalities, and points of view, and came home with what turned out to be almost 400 pages of transcribed text, enough for a production a week long. The weeding out of countless fascinating and cogent tales is horrible and painful and you think you can't do it, but you have to get a grip and let them go. After more tries with a framework than I'd like to admit (some with fourteen characters, one with two), I settled on portraying six women, to give a range of the many perspectives without being overwhelming about it: three Jews and three Palestinians, each based on and named for real individuals, each using many of the woman's actual words, each quite different in character and nature from the others. In real life the women did not know each other; poetic license granted them strong relationships to one another in the monologue.

The main setting was a kitchen in the Jerusalem home of one of the Jewish women. She and another Jew, driven by the desire to have the complexities of their history and perspectives on the conflict understood by Americans in more depth than the cold-blooded generalities of media allow, are directly addressing the audience. A third Jewish woman arrives, the cousin to one in the play (a stranger to both in real life) who has recently emigrated to Israel from the Soviet Union and whose views of the Palestinian problem are diametrically opposed to the others'. Hesitant to open up to the audience, she is pushed to defend her opinions about the Arabs. (These three characters are illuminated in more depth in the next chapter for their subtle energetic qualities.) Three Palestinians appear as well, each in isolation from the others, also speaking their stories directly to the audience, fired by the knowledge that they are almost never heard. Each of the three Arab women was of a different place and background to give a sense of the many kinds of lives affected by the hostilities: one a frightened woman living alone in a farming village, one an angry mother in a crowded refugee camp, and one a dignified teacher of English in the city of Ramallah who worked with Israelis in the peace movement.

The *When*, therefore, was now. The *Where* was several places at once: the theatre where the performance was taking place (acknowledging the reality of the audience), also a Jerusalem kitchen, also three homes of the Palestinian women (separated from the kitchen by a circle of stones and indicated by one chair).

Because of how the stories were collected, the Jewish characters were more fully etched and their stories of greater length and detail. This was because on that journey to gather the stories, most of the Jewish women I met spoke English; we were bonded by our common Jewishness whether or not we agreed politically; and I was able to return easily to their homes for more extensive interviewing, so their stories could grow and expand. To meet the Palestinians, on the other hand, I had to enter the West Bank in risky and sneaky ways and needed guides and translators for each visit—young Arab men with their own agendas when a tape recorder was running. A Palestinian woman might be bent over in wordless sobs at her son's imprisonment, and I'd be hearing a translation about the number of children growing up without schooling or health care in refugee camps. These facts were important but sometimes had nothing to do with what my interviewee was actually saying. Further, most of the Arab women were under-standably wary of me: Why was I, an American Jew, wanting to talk to them? Was it dangerous to speak with me? Even when we became friendly, it was usually impossible to return to their homes for more information.

In the end, I came home with shorter stories and fewer personal details from the Palestinian women than I did with the Jews, an imbalance that significantly informed the design of the monologue. While the three Jewish characters jabbered, prepared a dinner, tore the issues apart from every angle, and argued at length in the kitchen—one storming out from the heat of disagreement—the Palestinians told their more concise tales in isolation from one another on a separate part of the stage. At the end of the piece, the two remaining Jews bemoan the fact that their Arab counterparts have not had the same opportunity to speak their truths. The feast they have taken the two hours of the performance to prepare, it turns out, is for the Palestinian women, that they may perhaps come inside and sit and eat and finally be heard more fully. And so the piece ends, not with a closure but with ongoing strain and some wishful thinking.

Although in this piece the stories were an edited version of the real women's own words, the framework and relationships were totally contrived, and the history of their land offered through the characters' mouths was an amalgam of many women's input.

WORDS

"It's the words that sing," wrote Pablo Neruda. "They have shadow, transparence, weight, feathers, hair, and everything they gathered from so much rolling down the river, from so much wandering from country to country, from being roots so long."

As monologuists we speak. We enter a character, handle a couple of props, move around now and then, juggle a little stage business, but mostly we trade in words. What we speak *of* (the content of the stories) may be the heartbeat of our work, but *how* we speak it (the nature and quality of the text) is the back of the beast on which the story is carried to the hearts of its listeners—or not.

It is unspeakably embarrassing to reduce the enormous topic of dramatic language to a small subheading of a chapter, but it's what's available. So just a few words about words, starting with what our grandmothers yelled when something unseemly fell from our young lips: *"Watch your language!"*

Watch your language. Always watch your language.

Our speaking into life the intricacies of a human soul with the hope of penetrating our common one, our going for the heart of the story that our hearts might be cracked open, requires words like finely chiseled stone arrows, words that aim precisely and pierce both heart and soul, words of flame and muscle streaming easily from tongue, throat, and belly.

I once heard a student ask a teacher, "How do I find my writer's voice?" And the teacher answered wisely, "You don't. Your voice finds you." True. Each of us will meet, wrestle with, and speak from a voice that finds us, but we need to go where we will be found, and we'd better prepare to live up to it when it taps us on the shoulder.

So though you will need to go elsewhere for concrete and detailed help with dramatic writing, I offer here a thimbleful of general advice. Read, read, and read more. Listen, listen, and listen again. Read not only drama—Shakespeare and the other masters, an obvious course of action—but read poetry, read novels, read the exquisite writing of many nonfiction writers, nature writers especially, read the autobiographies of lit souls who match the fire of their lives with the fire of their words. Read to expand your knowledge of the world, but read as well to swim in the waves of elegant and eloquent language. Read to fatten your vocabulary, read for a sense of the literal, living force and active energy of words finely chosen and rhythmically arranged. All dramatic speech is a form of action. In monologue we have the blessed space to be more descriptive as well, but still, it's language spoken with the intent of being heard, this minute, by those people, for a compelling reason, which turns the words into something active. Read for the music of sound, its slants of light, its moods, colors, tones. Listen to music itself for the textures and rhythms with which to drape your words.

We have become accustomed to the banal blather of characters in soaps, sitcoms, commercials, third-rate dramas, consistently dumbed down the better to be swallowed with no trouble, the way news anchors are required by their sponsors to dumb down their vocabulary to an eighth-grade level so that the show's commercials won't appear too stupid. In our own work, let us not condescend to ourselves, our stories, our characters, our audience by thinking it a fabulously clever thing to ape perfectly the mundane half-speech of our everyday lives, a dulled language that never speaks of our soul, but of the apathy, fractures, and distraction that obscure it.

In the tradition of the Tsutujil Mayans of Guatemala (as described in the scrumptiously worded books of Martín Prechtel)[3], delicious, ornate ritual speech is learned by the young and offered throughout one's life as food for the holy who are nourished by such eloquence when it is true and from the heart. In our own culture we have lost, if we ever had it, all reverence for the power and necessity of words used magnificently, which does not mean stilted poetic artifice, but language chosen for the musk, the salt, the sweat, the smoke, and the heat of our blood-pumping selves.

The language of honeybee is dance. When a bee finds a patch of flowers with some fabulous pollen way over there in that field half a mile past the red barn, he flies back to the hive and dances out directions to the treasure. And if the pollen is extra-specially fine in that one patch of clover, the dance becomes all the more ecstatically ornate to describe it.

The language of *our* dance is words. Here are a few to remember as you conjure the language to hold the drama that holds the story that holds the questions that hold us together:

"Find a way to make beauty necessary.
Find a way to make the necessary beautiful."[4]

---

[3]Prechtel, Martín. 1998. *Secrets of the Talking Jaguar.* New York: Penguin Putnam; Prechtel 1999. *Long Life, Honey in the Heart.* New York: Penguin Putnam; Prechtel 2002. *The Toe Bone and the Tooth.* London: HarperCollins.
[4]Michaels, Anne. 1996. *Fugitive Pieces.* New York: Vintage Books.

6

Character

AN AFFAIR OF THE HEART

"Every individual," wrote Herman Hesse, "represents the unique, the very special and always significant and remarkable point at which the world's phenomena intersect, only once in this way and never again." So too every character we create. Your character is the "unique, special, significant and remarkable" presence and breath that gives life to the heart, blood, and bones of your monologue. Here all discussion of the mystery of human nature is a useless exercise; you must *enter* that mystery body and soul. You become it.

Whether a character is based on a living person, inspired by a historical figure, or totally fictional, it has, if it's rich and complex, a subtle body, and you can move into certain patterns and vibrations of this field so that your portrayal sings its music and illumines its once-only spirit.

But please note: The use of subtle energies as described in this chapter is not a replacement for the essential aspects of character development you'll learn elsewhere. It's neither the purpose nor within the scope of this book to include those fundamental physical, vocal, emotional, and imaginative acting tools, but they are the indispensable ground which give meaning and value to the work which follows, and without that base, matching the character's configuration of subtle energies, however sensitive and accurate it may be, is like taking vitamins on an empty stomach, or watering a plant without soil in the pot.

What's offered here is a meaningful and powerful addition to that work, but it cannot serve as the whole process.

And even the "whole process" is not the whole process, for what we're doing with all these aspects of character is trying to get to that inscrutable essence of us that cannot be learned from classes or books. We're mapping the soul. Cartographers must know their territory before mapping it, but we work backwards: we etch our maps of a being—charting body, voice, behavior, objective, subtle energy—in the hope that it will *lead* us to the unmappable territory of spirit, far beyond latitudes and longitudes. In either case the map, necessary though it be, is not the territory.

Some theatre folks object to the very word *character* for what we portray: it's too static a term, they say, for the fluidity of real human nature. They're right. If I'd found a better word, I'd use it. A *character* in the *Oxford English Dictionary* sounds like something branded or stamped into us: "the sum of the moral and mental qualities which distinguish an individual or a race; the individuality impressed by nature or habit on man or nation." Indeed we do carry such ingrained *characteristics* in the personalities of self and culture. We're born with some, we acquire others from environment and experience. They're real, deeply impressed on us, and writers and actors observe and include them in their portrayals. But beyond that, our character and certainly its spirit are more elusive. *Spiritus* is the movement of breath, and we are made of myriad movements of change, connection, relationship, and transformation; it's our nature to be a surprise. Further, despite what modern culture would have us believe, we are not discreet, isolate beings disconnected from all else in the universe, which itself is alive and in constant flux.

Some weeks after New Orleans was almost obliterated in the aftermath of Hurricane Katrina, a woman who'd been trapped in the convention center told her story.[1] By then we'd all been inundated with reports of looting and shooting, even raping in the convention center. This woman, baffled and angered by such reports, spoke of how her time with those frightened, abandoned people deepened her faith in humanity. She described how all inside the building rose to the occasion (as those "in charge" on the outside did not), of how considerate, generous, and kind everyone was to others, and that in all her time there she heard nothing of anyone's harming anyone else. As for criminals,

---

[1]*This American Life.* National Public Radio. September 18, 2005.

she said, yes, there were criminals in there—guys who'd been street gang toughs before Katrina, the kind you wouldn't want to tangle with—scary guys. And you know what? she said. This is what they did in there: they went to check up on all the old people and the women with babies and found out what they needed. Yes, they looted, she said. They broke into stores and took food to bring back for the elderly, the babies, the mothers; the only other thing they stole were matching raincoats so they could recognize each other in the crowd. "I hadn't liked those guys before," she said. "But I'll never look at them the same again."

Part of the magic of character work is that mingling of deeply enmeshed qualities of personality and soul with our inherent resilience and capacity for change.

There are three primary ways to use qualities of a character's force field for performance:

1. You can choose one to three *constants* of subtle energy design as the *hum* of the character's individual song (e.g., a strong chakra, a powerful level of the field, a will-reason-emotion leaning) and hold to them throughout the piece.
2. Drama being drama, a crucible always of possibility and transformation, you become conscious as well of a character's field modulating in response to the goings-on of a story (i.e., an expansion or contraction, a relaxing or holding its breath, energies jumping inside or out of the physical body, a change in the field's color, temperature, or tone) and move into the broad brushstroke of subtle realignment for a period of time.
3. If a vivid and enduring transformation occurs within a character (it usually happens toward the end of a piece if at all), you can charge up an element of the field which had been given no particular emphasis before, as when any part of us transforms, so too does our field.

So as practice, you begin to observe others' fields closely. The aim is never a cool, objective diagnosis laced with the presumption that you're going to help heal the misalignments of that person or charac-ter. Rather it's analysis married to "a kind curiosity." God forbid it should be the goopy, I-am-holier-than-thou kind of kindness, may it rot in hell, as Rose Solomon would say. Rather a fierce, respectful kindness infused with raw, unabashed wonder. We wonder for one thing what this person's story will tell us about our own. We wonder while observing what it means to be human. The *intention*, therefore, with which we perceive is of the essence.

Once I participated in a healing exercise that illumines the issue well.[2] Two students left the classroom with the teacher who explained that they'd return three times to stand before the group, each time thinking a different thought. They were not to express that thought in body, face, word, or behavior: just think it. The rest of the class was instructed simply to notice their feelings and sensations each time the students stood before them.

The first thought was: "There's something wrong with you and I'm here to fix it."

The second: "Whatever is wrong with you, I'd like to help."

The last: "I am curious to know more about you."

The class responded to both the first and second thoughts by feeling constricted, ill at ease, self-protective, and antsy. For the third thought, however, "I am curious to know more about you," they'd felt expanded, trusting, open, and relaxed.

All this from just the *thoughts* (which, remember, are themselves palpable, vibrational forces) of condescension or respect.

Of course you might be working on a character like Iago, Imelda Marcos, or Hermann Goerring, for whom great gobs of kindness and respect are not in the air—but curiosity is. And wonder about *how* and *why*. Michael Chekhov taught that actors must somehow love *all* our characters, the good and the evil, a St. Francis or a Hitler. Not always a breeze. Those college professors who advise their students to take acting as a fluff course in the midst of more "demanding" classes should only try it.

The *kindness* one needs when observing a real person's field or developing one for a character is not to be confused with foggy lack of discernment; and the *respect* is a bowing without the scraping. If you're hellbent on donning rosy-colored glasses and "honoring only the goodness in everyone," you'll miss the knife-sharp edges, the grit in the corners, the gaping holes, the warts, the mind-crunching complexity of us all, and thereby you'll miss the point. And too there is that other blade of kindness scraping at the edges of our sensibility, which Naomi Shihab Nye speaks of in her poem "Kindness":

---

[2]Exercise created by Susan Gallagher Borg, Resonant Kinesiology Training Program.

Before you know kindness as the deepest thing inside,
You must know sorrow as the other deepest thing.[3]

WHAT TO LOOK AND LISTEN FOR

There are specific things to consider as you look for what to work with
in a character's subtle body configuration. If you're creating the character from a person you have met, you of course have a lot going for
you. You will often expand, exaggerate, shift, or realign some of the
energetic qualities to better suit the stage, but there's the benefit of
reality to get you going. If you're developing the field of a fictional
character, it's helpful to arrive at the body and voice of that character
first, so you can sense the subtle energies manifesting in matter, rather
than simply imagining them in a disembodied way (although that is
possible, especially because it seems to be true that the nature of the
subtle body precedes and informs the formation of the physical).

You'll never need to perceive, enter, or portray *all* the following
qualities, but give yourself a wide spectrum to look for.

- *Direction of energy emphasis*: up or down, forward or back, within or
  outside the body, or relatively balanced throughout.
- *The quality of energetic cohesion*: scattered and erratic energy, or
  smooth and integrated?
- *The most prominent of the three leanings*: reason, emotion, or will.
- *The one or two strongest levels of the field.*
- *The one or two strongest chakras.*
- *Color, quality, and texture of the subtle body.*
- *Strength or weakness of the subtle body as a whole entity.*
- *Places where the energy is leaking out.*
- *Relationship of the subtle body to the physical.* Is this person "in his
  body" or "out of his body?" Is he "beside himself?" Do the
  energies seem to fly upward or forward or back?
- *What kind of music does your sense of the energies remind you of?*
- *Metaphors and images*: A given field may suggest a dreary, rainy
  day, bright sunlight at dawn, a strong oak tree, the bottom of a
  swamp, a volcano waiting to erupt . . . All such images reflect
  subtle but literal vibration.

---

[3]Nye, Naomi Shihab. 1995. *Words Under the Words*. Portland, Oregon: The
Eighth Mountain Press, from "Kindness." p. 42.

- Note as well *how the person makes you feel:* Tired? Inspired? Depressed? Hopeful? Sucked dry? Filled up? What is the beating of field on field? What is the nature of that *something* in this person you can't put your finger on but which radiates strongly?

When observing a real person's field, rarely will your understanding of the subtle energies come from your literally *seeing* the field. Once in a while you may be so blessed, but don't count on or worry about it. Mostly you will deduce the subtle energies' patterns, qualities, and movements from what's right in front of your eyes and ears—the nature of

- language,
- voice,
- physical body (bearing, shape, movement, mannerisms, rhythms),
- ways of relating to you and all else,
- thoughts, emotions, and their expression,
- the actual content of the person's story, and
- the mystery of that particular manner or style of presence.

When you're creating a fictional character, it's a similar process: as you develop the body, behavior, language, voice, personality, and story, you begin to sense, understand, and move into the essence of the invisible force field that's been informing those qualities to begin with (informed itself by forces *beyond* it).

Think about which energetic qualities strike you most forcefully about a character. *You need to use only one or two, occasionally three.* If you combine too many, the view you create may be muddy. It's like using accents for the stage; if you speak in the actual way a person from that region speaks, the audience might not understand you. You have to isolate and incorporate a few of the accent's qualities and leave the rest alone. To bring the spirit of the character both colorfully and comprehensibly to life, choose the *notes* of energy that are brightest and most resonant. Complexity of personality is something always to strive for; complicatedness of portrayal is not.

LANGUAGE

Character or real person, one's manner of language is part of the story that lives in the field. When creating a character from the ground up, it's helpful for the speech to emerge from that character's physical and subtle bodies. (Unless it's the speech of a real person you have been drawn to first, in which case you open the door of the body-field with that key.)

The following exercise begins with moving into character through physical qualities, from there discovering elements of the subtle field, and then allowing the language to arise from both.

Please note: Before all the exercises in this chapter, you'll need to review the descriptions and start doing the exercises in Chapter 3, the groundwork these practices depend on.

EXERCISE: LANGUAGE FROM THE BODY AND THE SUBTLE BODY

1. *Learning Someone Else's Walk*

Moving into another's walk is something actors do all the time both as practice and in evolving a character. Learn someone's walk in any way you choose, either with a partner helping you pick up the specific qualities in his walk as he models and describes it, or from secretly scrutinizing someone else's walk. Any individual's walk, however *normal* it may seem, is different from all other walks and carries elements of that person's story in its stride. Choose someone whose body and walk are noticeably different from your own. As you observe the person walking, look for distinguishing characteristics:

- How is the head held?
- Is there a bounce to the walk?
- What's the pace? The rhythm?
- How do the feet hit the ground?
- What are the arms and hands doing?

- Where are the eyes focused?
- How are the hips held?
- How are the shoulders held?
- Symmetries? Imbalances?
- Where's the breath?

There is no judging or analyzing involved! As you try on the preceding qualities and move them into your own body, what you feel is not a statement about the walker's reality. A short, plump person from Queens inhabiting the walk of a tall, lean person from the prairie is going to feel different inside the walk than the original walker. So be it. Learn the walk well. Notice its effect on you. Sense:

- How the configuration and movement makes your physical self feel: sluggish or enlivened or awkward or fluid, etc.
- What thoughts, emotions, and perspectives on the world the walk evokes.

- How it informs the placement, rhythm, and quality of your breathing.

2. *From Physical to Subtle Body*

- Practice that new walk for a bit, its stride, breath, rhythm, pace, bounce, rigidity, and sensations in your bones and muscles. Try its qualities standing, sitting, running, lifting things up, and putting them down.
- Now begin exaggerating it all just slightly. You're making a subtle step here away from the person whose walk you learned into a character inspired by the walk. Let your feelings follow the physical action. Find as many things to do in the room as you can, all within that new physical construct, all of it somewhat stretched into greater boldness from where it began.
- Begin noticing the subtle energies informing and informed by it all. Where is there most energy flowing to and from (energy emphases): head? butt? front? back? up? down? in? out?
- Do you feel an emphasis of one of the three leanings (reason, emotion, or will)? If so, how are you feeling it?
- What level of the field do you think is functioning most brightly? Why?
- Which chakra do you think is most powerful in this being? Why?
- Now set your attention on the area of the most prominent leaning or base coat, and heighten or brighten its pulse.
- Having thought about which field levels and/or chakras are strongest, begin tuning to and sensing what it feels like in your subtle body. With your imagination and intention, set your attention on the one level of the field you find most awake and radiant in the character emerging from this walk, and shift into its vibration. Keep moving in the exaggerated walk with a sense of this level's qualities surrounding and penetrating your physical being and magnifying it, informing what you do, think, and feel.
- While keeping that level of the field strong (and knowing you have moved into another persona from your original walking model altogether), focus on what you consider to be the most dominant chakra, and through imagination and intention heighten its charge, and flood it with its correlating color.

You may find certain elements of a field (either chakras or leanings or levels) easier to move into than others. Go for what's working for you right now and keep practicing the exercises in Chapter 3 to increase the possibilities. None of it happens overnight; proceed with patience and faith. You may choose to use the vibrations of two levels of the field, or two chakras, or one leaning and a color that infuses your whole body, either because it's what you can manage at the moment or because it's what suits the character best. Do what helps clarify the subtle energies most palpably for you and for the character. There are no rigid or immutable rules here.

- When you have fine-tuned these qualities of subtle energy to the best of your ability, move around a little bit more in their vibration and then, without letting them go, get paper and pen (or computer as a last choice) and sit down to write for the next part of the exercise.

3. From Subtle Energy to Language

The writing can be done immediately or later—but not so long that you aren't able to return to the body-field of the character inspired by the walk you learned. As you write, you must be inside the qualities of that body-field. Sense the particular qualities of subtle energy you are heightening and hold to the essence of the emerging character. You are writing, in other words, not only from the body of that character, but from having entered some specific qualities of her vibratory flow and patterns.

- Give yourself about forty-five minutes.
- For the first ten to fifteen minutes, draft out a character sketch and the given circumstances.

For the sketch, write down, in the first person, some facts about this character you've become; for example, "My name is Dora. I'm eighty-seven years old and grew up in a tenement in New York City. I hated my husband for no reason other than that he was short. Short people have always made me crazy. I myself am four foot ten, but strangely I have never hated myself. I always wear gray. It is my favorite color. My dream was to be a secretary and file things. I like knowing where things are, the smallest things, the things everybody else loses because they don't care about them. Small things are exactly what the world is built upon, and we need to know where they are so the world will not fall apart. . . ."

The important thing is not to think too hard about it; just write. Write from the being within the energy configuration, the body and the concomitant perspectives, and see where it takes you.

After drafting the sketch in the first person, conjure the given circumstances. They can be very mundane, as in, "Dora, who has always obsessed on keeping the small things in order, has lost her cat. She of all people would not lose a cat. She has always suspected the man next door to be a thief. She rings his doorbell." Or it could be a more dramatic moment: "Dora's husband, the one she has always hated because he is short, is dying. She thinks how cruel she's been to him, though he was a decent man and provided for her by slaving away. She wants to apologize to him but isn't sure if he's in a coma or can still hear her, which irritates her about him all over again. She sits by his bed in the hospital."

- Having written sketch and circumstances, now take half an hour to write a monologue for this character in the first person. (If you have more than half an hour, by all means continue; if not, stop wherever you are in the writing.)
- Read the monologue aloud in that character's voice, however it comes out of you. *Note the integration of body, subtle energies, language, and voice all working together.* If you're in a class, read the pieces aloud to each other.
- What do you note about this character's language: wording, rhythm, phrasing, fluidity, stumbling, humor, sobriety, etc? How does this manner of language and articulation differ from your own?

In choosing subtle energies to highlight for a character, you move toward *strengths* of the field rather than weaknesses, blockages, or absences. It's difficult to play a weakness or absence of anything, and it drains energy from a performance. Also, not all aspects of a field's strength are reflective of a strength in personality; what a heightened energy construct indicates depends on the workings of other elements in the field and in the story of that person. For example, if one has a highly charged will center and little energy running through the heart, you could end up with someone who forcefully accomplishes what he wants with no care for how it may affect others (blind ambition). Or it could be someone with a very strong third eye (chakra 6)—highly intuitive about others—who uses that ability solely for power and glamour. This doesn't mean you don't use that strength in your portrayal but that you understand its context and effect.

SENSING THE FIELD

Here are some clues for perceiving qualities of someone's field simply from what you see and what you hear.

SENSING THE FIELD FROM THE VOICE

1. *Outer Voice*

A person's voice includes the literal manner of speaking, the content of what is said, language style and choice of words, vocal patterns and rhythms, color, pitch, strength, and texture of speaking voice, accent or dialect, and from where in the physical body the voice is resonating. As you write your text, *hearing* the qualities of your character's speaking voice will guide the writing by the singular way language comes out of his mouth. Always read what you've written aloud in that voice to see how it feels in your body, mind, heart: how honest or fake, how alive or comatose. If you have the speaking voice down, you may find yourself *writing aloud* on occasion, discovering the text from what streams out of your/the character's mouth.

- Over time, study accents and dialects. Feel the vast differences of the way you look at the world when speaking with the music, rhythms, and resonance placement of another language. What does that music bring forth when superimposed on the English language? How does it change the energetic emphasis in your field?
- For a particular person, listen for (and always try it out yourself) where the voice resonates from in the physical body. This can be from bones, organs, interstitial tissues, fluids, spaces within or between any of those—anywhere throughout the body. (A foundation of good vocal training—far beyond the parameters of this book—is of the essence.) Deducing this place of resonance can be tricky. The voice may sound strong but scratchy, as if it's belted out from a contracted throat (which, if you try to act it from there, will give you laryngitis). As you come to know qualities of the person, you may feel that actually the voice is emanating from the

base of the spine. You're walking the edge here, as actors often do, between reality and metaphor. If it *feels* to you that the base of the spine makes sense, try it as the source for the voice, using attention, imagination, and intention to do it. If it works, the fact that the base of the spine connects with the root chakra may tell you something about how that person moves on the earth and integrates voice, body, and field. Or say someone's voice is intensely high-pitched and nasal, almost brash; not a beautiful sound, but up in the head as it is, it could be reflecting all sorts of things. Perhaps high energies of mental strength and acuity. Or it could be the voice of this person got shoved up into the back of the head from not having been listened to for an entire childhood. Maybe it's how the whole family has spoken for six generations. Who knows? Part of me wants to say, "Figure it out," and another part pleads, "Let it be." It's a delicate balance of the curiosity to understand and a delight in the mystery of it all, between the danger of pseudo-psychologizing (which serves no purpose) and acknowledging that whatever the story was, it is *living right now* in this being's voice and energies. The significant thing is that each person, each character, is a unique constellation of story and context, and the quality of spoken voice is part of a larger matrix.

■ Choose the place of vocal resonance that makes sense with your understanding of the character, and when you bounce your own voice from that place in the physical body (literally or figuratively), charge up the *subtle energies* there by imagining a brightness, or vibration, or color, or an enlivening image. There will be times when you know the placement is right, but don't know precisely what it signifies. Never mind. Just go for the resonance and the charging up, and whatever it means about this person will speak for itself.

■ The edge between metaphor and reality is tenuous at best, sometimes nonexistent. If this voice to you is hot summer wind, bottomless green ocean, sandpaper, blue taffeta, woodpecker on tin roof, believe in those images and take them directly into the texturing of your subtle energies, not as little quasi-poetic fantasies, but as realities deserving energetic expression. Follow the whole image or qualities of that image into your own field. Where does it live? What shapes, textures, temperatures, or colors does it urge your field to take? What is usable? What not?

■ There are qualities of voice that—given other elements of the story—give you a clear hit on qualities of the subtle body: wispy soft voices, loud and clear, stuttering or halting, full and embracing voices, *can* reflect directly a field that is in or out of the physical body in one fashion or another, or dim or brilliant colors in the emotional level of the field, or a vibrant sense of will and direction in the third chakra, etc. While avoiding glib assumptions, by all means take the hints and follow where they lead energetically, seeing if where you come to coheres with the rest of the story.

2. Inner Voice

One's Voice with a capital V is more than the vocal and verbal; it includes actions, perspectives, behavior, the things one creates, one's bearing, all reflecting the invisible field on one form or another.

■ Listen for the relationship of speaking voice to the Voice of the character's actions, behavior, and bearing. (In part, this bleeds over into sensing the field from the physical body, but it lives here too.) Sometimes the spoken voice works in harmony with the unspoken Voice, sometimes not. When not, there are times when the disjunction is itself harmonious within the person; other times it mirrors a discord. Always it points to our complexity and the tangles and streams of subtle energy intertwining. Is this someone for whom the two aspects of voice are in alignment, or is there a disjunction between what is heard and what you observe of thought, word, or action? You might be listening to someone whose speech is hesitant and awkward, yet whom you see to be refined, even regal, in his ways of carrying out what he needs to do or his ability to listen to others. The hesitancy and awkwardness may be a mark of restraint, a sense of privacy; there may be nothing hesitant or awkward about his thought and action in any other sense. So be careful of analyzing a quality of speech at face value without observing the whole. And be careful as well of observing everything else without listening to his speech! In this case, sort out what aspects of subtle energy might reflect the regality. A strong fifth level of the field (personal will aligned with universal will)? Or a powerful and expansive sixth level (unconditional love)? And how would you tune to the qualities of vocal hesitancy or privacy: one way would be a tough and self-protective energetic boundary, by choice not quite as permeable as it might be.

In Doris Kearns Goodwin's book *Team of Rivals*, there's a wonderful description of Abraham Lincoln's physical bearing contrasted with his manner of public speaking that illustrates marvelously the seeming discords of a Voice's expression.

> [Lincoln] plodded forward in an awkward manner, hands hanging at his sides or folded behind his back. His step had no spring. . . . He lifted his whole foot at once rather than lifting from the toes and then thrust the whole foot down on the ground rather than landing on his heel. "His legs," another observer notes, "seemed to drag from the knees down, like those of a laborer going home after a hard day's work."
>
> In repose, his face was "so overspread with sadness," the reporter Horace White noted, that it seemed as if "Shakespeare's melancholy Jacques had been translated from the forest of Arden to the capital of Illinois." Yet, when Lincoln began to speak, White observed, "this expression of sorrow dropped from him instantly. His face lighted up with a winning smile, and where I had a moment before seen only leaden sorrow I now beheld keen intelligence, genuine kindness of heart, and the promise of true friendship." Five minutes in his presence, and "you cease to think that he is either homely or awkward."[4]

With someone as multidimensional and complex as Abe Lincoln, or anyone else for that matter, you could, but do not *have* to, find the field's subtle patterns giving rise to the two *voices:* the ungainliness and the deep melancholy on the one hand, and the free exuberance of public speaking on the other. You might just do them physically, vocally, and emotionally—as is the usual magic of our brand of shape-shifting—and the elements of subtle energy will align accordingly. Or you could choose to change the density and hues of the field's vibrations according to the situation: a characterization of Lincoln might include his energy field's heaviness and downward emphasis at some points, and golden, sparkling expansive exuberance at others. In any event, for a character with as enormous a soul as Lincoln's, you would know at the least that all else would take place energetically within an exceedingly large, coherent, and powerful field.

---

[4]Goodwin, Doris Kearns. 2005. *Team of Rivals.* New York: Simon & Schuster. pp. 6–7.

SENSING THE FIELD FROM THE BODY

Much of the body's construct is genetic, which itself is a base note of one's story and field. But how one lives within that body, what radiates through it from the inside out, how its posture and movement reflect the person's attitudes, experiences, emotional life, spirit, and relation to the world, are all clues to the unique intricacies of what's going on in the invisible force field. Sometimes it's explainable, and sometimes it's not. And that's life.

As with learning another's walk, it's best to *experience* the workings of that body in your own to arrive at a sense of what's happening energetically. You take another's walk, stance, mannerisms, rhythm, and posture, and stretch toward a sense of that body's shape, even if it's different from your own: its lightness or heaviness, briskness or sluggishness, hardness or softness, strength or weakness. Is there a collapsing of the chest? Strong muscular arms and spaghetti legs? A massive torso and frozen pelvis? Swinging hips and bouncing gait? All of this is part of your usual training.

But then consider the physical body as the densest and slowest vibrational level of the force field, a reflection on a visible level of what is taking place in the higher frequencies of energy. A forceful upper body and thin or de-energized lower body might speak to a powerful will center (or a job at a lumber mill) and an ungrounded root chakra. A frozen pelvis could speak to something awry in the energy center having to do with sensuality and sexuality (chakra 2), or it could be from a car accident. The strength and grace of a body might speak to the power of the first level of the field. All of these observations are significant, and none of them mean beans without the broader story.

I once read a book about a woman who was totally paralyzed from birth and unable to communicate in any way. She was shunted from one home for the mentally impaired to another her whole childhood and neglected in all the homes thereafter, considered "retarded," until one nurse gradually discovered the woman's perfectly functioning mind. The book was written by the woman herself, one letter at a time through glances of her eyes at a board of letters, and revealed a person with one of the strongest wills and fiercest hearts imaginable. Most of her field was not, in sum, reflected anywhere in her physical being. We look for hints, clues, guesses, and guidelines, and they matter profoundly; but in the end, we must see how they are woven within their context.

STORY AND FIELD

A person's story itself, as explained in Chapter 2, lives inside the fabric and flow of the subtle body. Sometimes one energetic pattern with which you illumine a character will have to do with a specific moment in her story, and another with an ingrained personality trait. Seeing someone in action at any given time, especially a time of heightened challenge or for that matter delight, will not necessarily point accurately to that person's ongoing makeup; initially you may not know whether she was born with those qualities and has carried them all her life, or whether they've been brought up by circumstance. The tango of what you came in with and what your story demands of you is so intensely cheek to cheek, you can't always tell who's leading. Knowing as much of the context as you can helps you clarify energetic choices, and helps you know when you need to shift them into another pattern or emphasis.

Consider the character of Oskar Schindler who'd been an unimaginative ne'er-do-well, an alcoholic womanizer, and a Nazi sympathizer. Yet during the worst of the Nazi horror, Schindler found within himself a blazing core of courage, compassion, conviction, and creative will, through which—at enormous risk to himself—he saved from extermination thirteen hundred Jews whose children and children's children honor him to this day. No one knows why or how he rose to this heroism. Interestingly, after the war years, he was never able to find himself or his direction again. No judgment there. He did more good in a few years than most of us will accomplish in ten lifetimes. Just a wonder once more at the secrets and mazes of our human soul. Not having studied Schindler, I don't know what parts of his energy field one would use in characterization, but clearly its strengths, shape, and manner of flow would shift and change within the progress of his story.

There are others, in contrast, whose natures are constant throughout their stories' landscapes and help define the terrain. Maria von Maltzan, the German countess mentioned previously, also saved many Jews during the Nazi era. Like Schindler, she risked her life repeatedly to help others in ingenious, chilling, and sometimes hilarious ways. But von Maltzan came onto the earth with a flaming, willful, brave nature already intact, and learned from her father to use it to help those less fortunate than she. Her one brother became an ardent member of the Nazi Party, while she loathed, mocked, and fought everything to do with the Nazis right from the beginning.

The Countess' character shines through the stories of her childhood, such as the one below, which foreshadow her later escapades as a member of the anti-Hitler Resistance.[5]

THE COUNTESS

[Speaking to a journalist with a thick and uniquely flavored German accent]

I was raised in a castle. It was called Militsch. 18,000 acres, 93 rooms. Not 94—93, get it straight. Oh ja, it was wonderful. At Militsch we had every-thing: elks, wild pigs, deer, snakes. As a child I found snakes wonderful. . . . I find snakes so pretty. My sisters were too stupid to find them pretty. Na ja, poor little snakes, they don't have any legs. And the Bible was horrible about snakes. All my life I've not been frightened of lots of things that other people are frightened of. I'm not frightened because I See *it. What is there to be fright-ened of? My brother was frightened of snakes—Dear Little Boyzie—He was frightened of everything, but he was deadly frightened of snakes. . . . One thing I will never forgive him is The Great Snake Slaughter.*

In our park there were many snakes: grass snakes, Blinschleichen, Addern. *There was a bridge, and there I would leave for the snakes a saucer of milk. Snakes have no hearing, but they always knew when I was coming because they could feel on the bridge the vibrations of my feet, and then they would come to meet me. Close by they were even prettier. One day I came home from school, and I saw packs of dead snakes lying in rows. I was furious! I asked the gardener what happened. He said, "Your mother ordered it because your brother the count, the horrible little count, is frightened of snakes." I was . . . I was . . . I can't tell you how furious I was! I nearly drowned my brother. Nein, it was quite a good effect for him. I got him into my boat and gave him a little push and held his legs. Quite effective.*

Oh na ja, my father wanted me to apologize and give to my brother a kiss of peace. I said, "I'd sooner eat the vomit of a stranger!" (Pause) *I was always rather drastic about such things.*

Nein, it's not very difficult to drown someone. I tried once to drown the King of Saxony. He wanted to disturb some birds who were trying to mate. I threatened him with drowning. He looked down at me and asked how I could

---

[5]Lust, Marianne. 1995. "You Do What You Do." Unpublished. pp. 8–10.

do this. So I explained it to him in great detail. He thought I was quite fine!
(Pause)

Dear little Boyzie. It gets me absolutely sick that someone would kill what they are frightened of. It is a terrific cowardice. One must always stand for the weaker.

Many years later, von Maltzan's repeated defiance of the Nazis revealed the same outrageously determined character. One time, two vicious members of the SS tore apart her apartment trying to discover the Jews they'd been informed she was hiding. Though she denied their accusations as if grossly insulted, she did in fact at that moment have two Jewish men, one of them her lover, concealed in a large fold-out couch. The Nazis tried in vain to open the couch, and when they couldn't budge it ("I had put hooks on the inside," she explained, "which only the people in there could open."), they were suspicious. The Countess continues in the text:

"Look," I said, "if you don't believe me that there's no one hiding inside there, why don't you just take your pistols and shoot right into the couch. Go ahead! Shoot! Shoot! Uh, one thing only. Afterward, I'll have to have it reupholstered. So before you shoot, I want you to sign a paper saying that you'll agree to pay for the new material and the repair. I won't go about in a messed up flat just because you think someone's hiding in there."

What do you think? Nah, they were such perfect bureaucrats, they didn't dare sign this little piece of paper. To kill people was part of their job requirement. Furniture repair was not. Nah, what could they do. They just strutted about for a while in their stupid uniforms and then they left.

Playwright Marianne Lust and I visited the Countess in Berlin when she was old, her health failing, but her stubborn spirit as vital as ever. Even then, as I'd mentioned in another chapter, the force of her third chakra, her indomitable *will,* was evident in her speech, her behavior, and even the shape of her body, which was unusually thick and strong directly around the solar plexus. Also she had an unusually strong fifth Level of the field aligning her personal will with a greater universal will. Rather than tuning to that level of the field, I chose an image with which to perform her, to help me rise to her warrior self. Just before going on stage each night, I imagined draping her and myself in the bright red cloak of the Warrior Archangel Michael, and we moved, she and I, "dressed" in that cloak, into the stories of her holy battle.

SPIRIT AND FIELD

You observe real human beings, you see the multicolored, many-tex-
tured threads of self braided together into one being and how we, just
like the stories we inhabit, are beings of *paradox, contrast, flexibility,* and
surprise. Not surprise as in inconsistency, or contrast as in confusion. A
random conglomeration of diverse qualities is not a character but a mess.
But as we come up with the traits of each character, we must lift them all
like rocks to view the underneath of what we thought we knew. Moment
to moment or in the same exact moment, a quality of character will suddenly sparkle in the light of its other side: courage washed by vulnera-
bility, compassion chilled by the same character's icy wind, a wild and
raucous humor leaping out of the soberest soul. The braiding together of
a character's diverse traits adds up to more than the sum of its strands.
The inexplicable mix of self is part of that unmappable part of us.

We cannot literally observe the quality of one's spirit as we do a
walk, a voice, a body, a mannerism, and usually we don't have the
vocabulary to trap its essence. Even the most complete and profound
comprehension of the workings of our subtle energies, and all the skill
in the world to match their frequencies and arabesques of pulse and
light, will not provide for us in character work an answer to the riddle
of how and why our mottled spirits sing or soar or sink. But we can *feel*
the spirit of another, we can *know* its presence and meet it with the wisdom of our own. We'll sense a warrior soul, an uncommonly compassionate or love-washed soul, a soul in true, even mystical connection
with all that's humming on the earth. Those are grand and rare and
splendid ones, to be sure, but we will recognize the milder versions
too, and every conceivable face of spirit between.

Though our subtle bodies are neither the only nor the deepest
dimensions of our nonmaterial selves, they are a potent and highly
nuanced intersection of matter and spirit. The three highest levels of
the force field's vibration (spiritual) connect with the three lower levels
(embodied) at the heart. So one's capacity to open to and match the
fifth, sixth and seventh levels of the field (higher will, unconditional
love, and relationship to spirit and the integration of the whole) is
worth developing for opening to those terrains of character. Moving
into these higher frequencies is not, alas, a matter only of will, intention, and diligent practice, though they play a big role in getting there.
Each successively higher level reflects and allows for a more complex

and comprehensive state of consciousness with which to perceive, hold, and connect to self, other, and world. Coming into those levels requires, for one thing, building the strength and clarity of your physical body as a container for holding the higher energetic frequencies. (See the bibliography for books with specific exercises to strengthen body in relation to field.) In the long haul, it asks of us as well a willingness to wrestle with the integrity of our own psyches, hearts, and spiritual courage. How easily said. How long and difficult the path of doing it. And how dishonest what we're taking on without it.

So one expands the field and increases its vibratory rate according to the particular quality of a character's spirit. You can use potent images as well (always through attention, imagination, and intention), like that red cloak of the warrior archangel draped around the German Countess, herself a holy warrior in the battle for justice. What such an image concretely means to you, the fire it lights within your own spirit, will literally create a frequency of its own —but only if that meaning is true and the fire is real. When an image is a fleck of intellectual cleverness or even brilliance resting in your intellect alone and not in your heart or soul, the constructs of the subtle body that will be illumined and charged are those having to do with your intellect, not necessarily anything else.

Tuning to a frequency, charging up an energy center, moving into a level of the field, or matching in vibration one image or another does not require a hundred and one *new* exercises. Keep going over and refining the same old exercises from Chapter 3, the ones you were allowed to skip over once upon a time. If you become as adept at these few as you can, the possibilities will expand, especially when added to that teeny little point about working on your own entire self for your own entire life. In the end it is your whole self turning somehow into poetry, becoming music, knowing that you're the mist rising from that mountain, and that you live between the lines of myth, and none of it is graspable and all of it is where our soul begins to speak.

EXAMPLES OF CHARACTER AND FIELD

In the last chapter I used a monologue about Palestinian and Israeli women as an illustration of structuring your drama. I offer now, from the same monologue, thumbnail sketches of three of its characters and the choices of energetic constructs used for each. All three were based on real women, most of their own words intact, though vastly edited. They are the Jewish women cooking and gabbing in a Jerusalem kitchen. One reason for choosing these particular three over the many I interviewed was the vivid contrasts between their bodies, voices, and subtle energies, and too because these three ordinary women with their coffee cups, their mousy dresses, their baggy sweaters, their jokes, insights, opinions, and quirks, were all holy warriors of sorts, each in her own distinctive way.

1. Brurya

A teacher, about 60, Brurya had been born in Palestine before it became Israel. She grew up proud of the idealism of her people to create a new life in this land, and fought in the War of Independence and subsequent Israeli wars, convinced (as she'd been told) that these wars were necessary to protect the Jews and their land. "Later," she said, "I became a cynic about all of it." About 250 pounds, she wore elegant black velvet pantsuits with ratty old sweaters around her shoulders, her long gray hair pulled back straight. She was a beautiful and powerful woman in her no-nonsense way, and her exceedingly low-pitched voice, smothered in its thick Hebrew accent, came straight out of her thighs. There was a sense of stone in her—not impenetrable stone; on the contrary, singing stone: stone that is the bone of the earth and has held in its marrow the songs and stories of centuries, millennia.

Brurya was a member of Women in Black, a group that demonstrated weekly in downtown Jerusalem against the Israeli occupation of Palestinian lands. The first time I met her, she said, "These demonstrations in the hot sun and the people cursing at you—you think I like it? Ha! I would like to close my eyes and take a nap and forget the whole thing. But I'll tell you one reason I can't. Because my youngest son, my baby, he's nineteen—a musician, isn't that nice?—tomorrow he goes into the army. And he doesn't want to go. He hates it. But he has to go. So that's my problem, you see, because the time between my wars and his war—ach. I went to my war like a dancer! I thought, *I am going to do great things for my people.* But my son, he hates this warring. He hates the whole thing—and I can't blame him. It never ends! 'I don't want to kill anybody!' he says. 'I don't hate the Arabs!'

"Why do they have to go and fight? It makes me crazy! What for? Another piece of land? I don't *need* that land. I love it, but I don't need to *own* it, to *rule* it! It should have been finished years ago already, and the whole thing makes me completely furious!"

Brurya's massive body was rooted in the dry, stony earth of her country. Her first words to me about her childhood were of the hot desert sand and her small feet burning as she walked across it. Her stories were peppered throughout with the idea of *home* for the Jews, and *home* for the Arabs. Her root chakra was wide open, charged, and bright; you could feel her rising up out of the very ground of Israel's joys and sorrows. Not all large people are automatically grounded. But she was, moving always with slow deliberation. Though an extremely intelligent and analytical person with a lot of energy in and around her head, even more obvious (in her build, her face, her words) was her tough, elastic heart—big and strong enough for the whole gamut of emotion to ride through like wild horses and not tear it apart. (It is Brurya who told the story of the Arab taxi driver in Chapter 1.)

For Brurya's characterization, I heightened and used the following aspects of subtle energies:

- the root chakra as connected to a very large, dense field, strongest and most alive on the lower half of her body, and
- the heart chakra: her fierce, open, angry, grieving heart, able to hold in its chambers a wealth of rage and compassion for both sides of the conflict, which roiling tension brought a heap of heated energy to the center of her chest.

2. ROSIE

I met Rosie as she too demonstrated on behalf of Palestinian rights. A microbiologist in her fifties, she had a quick, birdlike energy, most of it shooting up all around the top part of her body and forward, toward whatever she had to confront or communicate. Her shoulders were hunched a little forward, following her energy into whatever situation presented itself or demanded attention. Her voice was nasal and high, her hands quick and always busy. I was puzzled at first by the bizarre blend of accents in her speech, but her story explained it.

Born a Sephardic Jew in Bulgaria, Rosie grew up speaking both Spanish and Bulgarian. Her family was well-to-do: "We lived in the beautiful city of Sophia, and we had maids. We had a car, yes, a car. This was a very unusual thing in Bulgaria in those days, but what can I tell you—we lived well."

Rosie was a child when the Holocaust began and remembered clearly the slow process of the Jews' dignity, possessions, rights, and homes being taken away, and their ending up in a miserable ghetto where she watched her father being sent off to hard labor. Because Bulgaria had been an ally of Germany,

"Eichmann took his quota of 20,000 Jews from other areas Bulgaria controlled, not from Bulgaria proper. And those Jews, they all went to . . . they all burned. All we knew is people went to Poland, and it's very bad to get there. Like I mean we didn't want to go! But we didn't know the real story. And after the war, a few came back. And they told stories. One woman, she had a piece of soap in her hand. She said, 'You know? This was human!' So that was my childhood. Horrible."

When the war ended, the Communists took over Bulgaria, making life particularly hard for those who had been affluent before the war. Rosie's family decided to start life anew in Israel.

"Ben Gurion, he sent this old boat from Israel, and every month it came forth and back, forth and back, each time it took 4,000 of us Jews to Israel. So we went! We had nothing. Absolutely nothing. But I took my accordion; I thought it was all great fun, a real adventure."

Her family began their lives all over again in floorless huts on the treeless mud of the new land, trying (and failing) to learn farming:

"I learned English and Hebrew in one year; I was terrific. I mean, you know, terrific! It was the time of the Arab riots. The slaughters were so terrible. If I explained to you in detail, you would leave this room to be sick."

Eventually she came to study in the United States, and married an American man: "We lived in New York City for fifteen years, and it was the sixties—THE SIXTIES!—I had my consciousness completely raised!" Finally, she returned to Israel with her husband to support her people: "The Jews of this world, we have always been the underdog, and I am on the side of the underdog. . . . But then I come back, I look around myself, and I see—it's not so simple, who is the underdog."

By the time I met her, Rosie of the sharp mind, feisty will, and the capacity to start life over again and again with gusto, had become a committed activist for peace and Palestinian rights. As she told me her stories in her home, she sat, stood, showed me around her newly renovated house, answered the phone, jumped up to make more coffee, and never stopped talking throughout. She was both bursts of breeze and a bird on those breezes—a small, tough bird, like the intrepid chickadees who overwinter in Vermont in the bleakest and coldest weather.

Of her subtle energies, I emphasized

- her strong will, charging up Chakras 2, 3, 4, and 5 along the back— for the will leaning:
- a bright upward energy in and around her neck and head, her quick, bright mind, and
- a quickly pulsing field all round of crackling, sparkling energies—like twinkling stars or silent fireworks.

3. ALLA

In her mid-thirties, Alla had emigrated to Israel from the former Soviet Union with her husband and small children. A laboratory scientist, she'd been a *refusenik* in the USSR (a Jew punished for trying to emigrate to Israel), and to her own surprise became a human rights activist there. Small and fine boned, her soft voice and slightly mousy looks belied her steel will and unbending perspectives in her hatred of the Arabs. She was not a fanatic acting from a marble slab of abstract ideology; her emotional resistance to Arab rights, however tragic, had sprouted from the earth of her own story. In her quiet, gentle voice with its delicious Russian accent, she said, "My mother was a survivor of three concentration camps: Auschwitz, Maidanek, and Bergen-Belsen . . . And all her family were killed in these camps—All. And when she became at last free, she choosed to go to Russia . . ." where she met and married Alla's father who disappeared when Alla was one. They lived in anti-Semitic Yalta, and she and her mother were harassed and beaten in the streets. So they stayed inside as much as they could. "And in those nights alone together, starting when I was maybe five, my mother told me her stories. Which she never told to anyone else, only to me. She told me everything what had happened to her inside the camps. I remember them very clear." And she tells the harrowing stories.

"In Russia," she then continued, "I fought so hard for the human rights. If I were living anywhere else, I would be working for the people without the rights, because I believe it is the most important thing. But I am here. And in Israel, I must join with the people who protect *my* rights. . . . From when I was a little girl I came to hate the people who want to kill. That is all. There is nothing to discuss. Because you cannot cause pitiness out of these people. You cannot make them to pity. And I know this because I know how the German people and the Polish people, they saw the great crowds of Jews going to their deaths, and they did nothing. They felt no pitiness. They did nothing to stop it! So one day I grow up and inside me I become strong. I choose to defend myself. . . . You have to be very hard in order to survive. Very hard. . . ."

The harsh bitterness of Alla's story rubbed dissonantly against the fragile gentleness of body and voice. I chose three subtle energy characteristics.

- The light blue sheath of level 1 of the energy field wrapped tight and close about her like a shawl, for security and protection,
- A steely, straight line of intention running up and down her spine,
- A low, slow fire in her belly.

What one could focus on in such a character are the tears in the field, the hollows and leaks and bruises of pain and victimization. But that on its own takes you into a place from where there is no climbing out. The words, voice, and behavior of the character will carry that pain. What you want energetically is to ask, What is the ladder that has helped this woman climb far enough up from that hole of suffering to be able to look up, crawl out, and stand? In Alla's case, her powerful grid of first level energies were holding body and soul together compactly. Her hatred of those "who wish to kill" and "who have no pitiness" burned as a contained fire of determined self-protection in her center. And although that eternal flame carried potential harm to others, for Alla it was warmth in the face of the cold and icy places in her field where her own and her mother's stories had been frozen for years.

In a monologue with more than one character, learning to leap quickly from one frequency or subtle configuration to another, making character shifts sharp and invisibly profound, adds a rich texturing, a sense of contrasting melodies: human song lines crossing each other on the map. And it is a way, like music, of a character's presence filtering right through the skin of the listeners with a penetrative grace.

It is worth noting that we often carry in our own fields the energetic designs of parents, grandparents, and ancestors. We inherit some of the subtle energetic constructs they lived within—some delightful, some crazed—but unlike the physical attributes we also inherited, we are freer to reorient the energetic flows of subtle energies no longer working for us. Generations of women in a family may struggle with depression, handed down from field to field, though the initial reasons for it (perhaps oppressive and poverty-stricken lives in the Old World or backbreaking struggles in the New World) are long gone. Or you may carry a vinegar-and-pepper sense of humor that lives right inside your field, its way of being in the world inherited from forebears who developed it to survive with souls intact. The life-giving, subtle patterns we can be grateful for; the murkier ones we can break out of if we choose. In the case of character, you may know, deduce, and apply ancestral echoes living in the field. But of course in that case, it's never about deciding a character ought to maintain or break free of an energetic pattern; however it may have evolved, it's an integral part of the story right now.

CHARACTER AND HOME

One last word on creating character—from any place, of any time and any culture—to sing our human soul.

We are reminded today by many wise ones of what has been a centuries-long amnesia: our forgetting that our human nature cannot be understood in the context only of itself. Environmentalists (A friend says, "Oh get rid of that word; let's call them 'sane reverent people!'")[6] tell us that a California condor in captivity, "saved in a cage," is not really a California condor unless we would define one as "a feather-crusted bundle of meat. But if your concept of condor includes the animal's context, then it hasn't been saved at all."[7] In other words, part of a creature's identity is its environment. We forget it of the condor; we forget it of ourselves.

It is our modern way to probe the depths of the human soul by ripping our understanding of that soul straight out of the world that gives it life, substance, and meaning. "Our human meaning is no longer coordinated with the meaning of our surroundings. We have disengaged from that profound interaction with our environment that is inherent in our nature."[8] Another topic for another book.

And here we are at this crossroads in time, in part because of that very forgetting, looking for the road that leads to remembering.

---

[6]Casey, Caroline. www.visionaryactivism.com
[7]Jensen, Derrick. 2002. *Listening to the Land*. Quote of Neil Everndon. San Francisco: Sierra Club Books. p. 120.
[8]Berry, Thomas. 1999. *The Great Work*. New York: Bell Tower. p. 15.

Though we cannot speak the languages of other forms of life, we can and must listen—not only to hear and honor their own stories, but for what they can teach us about our own. Like all story gathering, it is not a matter of grabbing what we can get, scribbling it in a nature journal, and going home. The song in our shared story sings of an intimate, infinite, and inextricable relationship to all that exists, and of knowing that "All the stories that surround us are in us" refers not only to human stories.

So one last arpeggio—to be practiced over the course of at least one lifetime—for applying as you will to the creation of your characters that they might reflect richly and truthfully the story of who we are.

ARPEGGIO

Listen to the world, learning to perceive the subtle energies, physical qualities, *languages,* and *stories* of individual rock, wind, creature, weather, season, plant, landscape, insect, pond, or star. This practice is not a pleasant diversion from the real task at hand, but a necessary doorway to perceiving the subtle energies within the stories of our humanity. All beings are made of the same stardust; we all live or die by the absence or presence of the same life-force; we are all part of the same mystery; our human soul is bound to, enhanced by, and indebted to the souls of everything else. May we enhance in return.

For everything following, begin by centering, grounding, setting your intention, and becoming still, silent, and spacious.

- Go to a tree and *listen* to it in all the ways you can. Touch it, look at it, breathe its scent, lean on it, feel the energy inside it. Sense its subtle energy field. If you stand your whole body against it, what does it make you feel? Every species of tree has a different energetic flow. Some will ground and stabilize you; some will shoot your energy higher; some will comfort you; some will fill you up or make you feel fluid in the wind. Take in the bark, the leaves, the roots, the texture, the color, the weight, the smoothness or roughness, the toughness or flexibility, the width and the height, the way it reaches to stroke the cheeks of the clouds, bends toward the earth, rustles in the wind. Stay by it for a while and take it— literally—in. Read about that kind of tree. Empty yourself of preconceptions and labels. "This is an oak, it's tough. This is a maple; its sap makes syrup." Drop the labels and the preconceptions and just take in what's in front of you, beside you, against you, beneath you, around you.

- See if you can match any of its qualities with your own subtle energies, not to *become* the tree, but to sense that tree's essence within your humanness.
- Do the same with other trees and with flowers, mountains, fields, streams, frogs, blue herons, water bugs . . .
- Sit on a large rock. Grow still enough to feel its hum, its song, and see if you can tune to it. Another rock from another geological formation and with different stories carried in its belly will have a different force field.
- Listen to the energies of different times of day: the dark stillness before first light, dawn, midday, late afternoon, dusk, and midnight. Each carries its own force field; each evokes different responses and possibilities from us. Try it as the seasons turn, noting the way the subtle energies of high summer affect the quality of your story as it's being lived right then. How does it differ from the way deep winter, or autumn, or the edge of spring, affect your field, your story, your dance?
- Practice whenever you can. Sometimes it will be for just a moment or so—taking in the way the clouds reflect the colors of the sunset, the feel of the air after rain, the glisten of dew on the grass, a tulip just before it blossoms into its fullness, a circle of ferns turning brown and dry in late August. Each has its own vibration. Each has its story. Each has a language of its own. How does each thing affect your own subtle body? Does it relax and open it? Strengthen it? Heighten it with a particular color or rhythm?

Ah, you say. I live in the city! Given that who we are is integrated with who and what the rest of the natural world is, it's unnerving that theatre training and theatre productions are geared primarily to cities. So first, try this arpeggio with human-made things: buildings, streets in the morning or at night, city blocks, and bridges, because they are real and they have become part of us too. And then go to a park, or to the country, and practice with the grass, the ocean, the sky, the cliffs.

- When working on a character, move beyond, "This character is *like* a tiger or a squirrel." Maybe he *is* tiger or squirrel. Listen for the fields of the animals and include their environments: the landscape, the weather, the beings who live with and around them. What tones of this ecology live as part of the character? Consider the character's own environment, the elements of the immediate world that have fed into and helped shape their subtle energies. Or consider a quality of that being which is not so much *like* a force of nature as *of* it; and bring yourself into the humming field of that life-form, its weave of energetic buzz and flow. Bring one element of the intricate energetic hum into the character's own field; see if it enriches and enhances that being's truth and presence.

Even when you do not directly wash a character's force field with something of the natural world (and rarely will you do it consciously), your own deepening connection to its myriad rhythms will inform all whom you portray in one wild, invisible form or another. It does not have to be a conscious application to your character's design as in a paint-by-numbers project. The more you learn to sing to and of the world, the more it will sing through you on a stage.

And so this chapter ends where it began, with the idea of crafting into being characters who, in bringing fearlessly to light whatever we uncover about our human soul, do so—in Hesse's words—as "unique, very special and always significant and remarkable points at which the world's phenomena intersect, only once in this way and never again."

7

CHAPTER

Performance

NELSON MANDELA, WRITING ABOUT HIS TWENTY-SEVEN YEARS imprisoned on Robben Island, tells of a punishing system set to crush the inmates' spirits and his doubt that any one of them could have resisted alone. The authorities' greatest mistake, he says, was in allowing the prisoners to remain together, for in their support of one another and in sharing the bits and shards of truth they could find out about the world beyond the island, they were granted strength, which collective quickening "multiplied whatever courage we had individually."

We too, now, here, in our grand and stumbling island of a country with so much organized to crush the spirit, need—however we can find it—to multiply our courage in order to move on. And in theatre there is sometimes the glistening possibility of creating a container for the gathering of holy sparks to en-courage us, a magical space where performer and audience come together in communion, sharing the bits and shards of the world's truths, both tragic and beauteous, in such a way that we sink more deeply into our shared humanity and are granted communal strength. It doesn't happen all the time in theatre, not even much of the time. But it is possible, and when it comes, it brings a kind of transformation with it. As we move into performance, there are a few things we can do to set the stage for such a possibility.

To begin with, we can transmute our habitual fear of the audience to love. "Impossible! We are exposed; they are hidden. We lay ourselves out on the line; they are the judges of everything we are and do. We are alone; they are (hopefully) many." The anxiety bangs away at our hearts, consuming its space and energy.

You start by conjuring a blurring and a fading of the barrier between the *you* and the *them*—that same trembling line between *I* and *Not I*. You shift your focus from what separates performer and audience, to what connects us at the core: the fact, for one thing, that all of us are walking within the Murky Unknown; all of us are wrestling with questions that will, if we let them, hold us together. There is no exercise for it, no nifty list of steps to follow. But at some point in dressing room or wings, you just remember the bigger picture; you conjure the Larger Story or a piece of it that breaks your heart, from its beauty or from its loss. You think of the sweet-singing loons dying from lead in the water, of the majestic polar bears losing their ice, of the 30,000 children who die every night from curable diseases while our pharmaceutical companies spend trillions on drugs to eliminate women's facial hair. You remember the sorrows and the craziness we have spawned, and you praise and pray for the miracles beyond us and within us.

It may sound a perfectly outrageous thing to do before walking onto a stage, to bring up thoughts that may distract and disorient you, but there is nothing like a broken heart to put things in perspective and keep you threaded to the wider world, lifted from your own immediate fears and self-absorption. You remember why you ended up here in the first place in this theatre on this night in this absolutely mad profession, and what it means to you and those who've come tonight to be able to feed together the bird that sings "the most beautiful song in the world." For like Mandela and his fellow inmates on Robben Island, we cannot do it alone. If we have prepared well and with fierce spirit, and if we are truly here to feed the bird, then it helps to remember that they, those fearsome ones in the darkened seats, in their willingness to listen to the song, have come here to do the same. So it's a good thing to honor them even before the performance begins.

In some cultures, the actors come onto the stage and bow deeply at the start of a performance. It's an exquisite custom. Our own is to bow at the end, sometimes forgetting what that bow really means. It means not, "I am eating up your applause like candy, more, more, more!" (Although there's that too, and more power to it.) But the act of *our* bowing to *them* is, when you consider it, an act of tough and lucid humility. It means, "Without you, all that I have done tonight and all that I have done to prepare for it is meaningless. Without you, my work is isolate and my efforts unfulfilled." It means, "Thank you for your open souls and ears." It means, "We're in it—in this theatre, this experience, this aching world—together; I bow to what you give and how you care." Depending on who you are, it is also a bow to the holy, to the spirit—beyond, greater than, and connecting us all—which has brought us here, encouraged something to happen, and infused us with whatever love or strength has moved between us for this time. For lonely though the work of monologue performance is, and by God it is lonely, in truth we have done none of it alone.

We can bow at the beginning of a performance as well, for all the same reasons and to create as we set forth a conscious meeting place between actor and audience at this small crossroads in time. It may not be your style or appropriate to the performance to bow on stage at the start. But you can take three honeyed seconds to bow in the wings before entering—bowing to all that is sacred in the world (including those who sit there in the dark, longing for beauty and goodness), to our common capacity for anguish, ecstasy, and change, to the relationship that is about to form between you, to the people whose stories you are telling, and to all whose voices have yet to be heard. A bow, whether at the beginning or the end, reaches always from the heart and through the permeable boundary between us.

"The mind," writes Jack Kornfield, "thinks of itself as separate. The heart knows better. As one Indian master put it: 'The mind creates the abyss, and the heart crosses it.'" Though we are not healers, and our audiences buy tickets for a performance, not a healing, still there's some strange sustenance in recognizing that both healing and theatre meet at the heart. "Acting," says performance maestro Bill Esper twenty times a day, "is not an affair of the head, it's an affair of the *heart*." And so it is, always. And it's more than an actor's rich capacity for a moment-to-moment free-flow of honest emotion; it's also the heart to love what you're doing, to love why you're doing it, to love those you're doing it for, and to love the world it's about.

"Love, it turns out, may be one of the most powerful physical forces in the universe."[1] Love as a face of the life-force itself, making the impossible possible, one blade of grass pushing up through 450 pounds of soil just from the love of life.

---

[1] Goldner, Diane. 1999. *Infinite Grace: Where the Worlds of Science and Spiritual Healing Meet.* Charlottesville, VA: Hampton Roads.

Healing happens, it is said, not from within the healer or client, but from the *quality of the relationship* between them. And so it is in our art as well. On the road toward performance you have struggled with your relationship to your own spirit and the questions it asks, your relationship to the world and the stories which pull you, your relationship to the people who tell you their stories, your relationship to the characters you create. Now the force field that arises from the joined energies of you, story, and audience rests not only on what you have brought to the stage, but also on the brief, deep relationship between you and those who come to hear. We may as well love them—that faceless crowd we're accustomed to fearing—and if we do, we will significantly transform the vibration of the field we create together.

Once I was watching two American ice-skaters in the Winter Olympics on television. One of them had won two medals in the last two years. He came onto the ice determined to win again; you could see the force of will in his muscles, his face, in the sheath of steely energy around his whole body. The camera scanned the crowds in the bleachers, all holding their breath and biting their lips, the skater's father with rigid back and a jaw set in cement. The man skated out onto the ice wrapped in the force of his will, and somewhere in the middle of it all, he fell. And even though he got up and kept skating, that was the end of that.

The second skater had never been in the Olympics, much less won a medal; he was, in fact, a young lawyer who happened to skate as well, and it seemed not to occur to him that he might or should win anything. When he glided onto the ice, he was smiling from the sheer pleasure of it, his field clear, bright, and open. He looked around at his enormous audience, and you could tell he loved them too: "How good of you to stop by!" With nothing to lose, he skated in a literal glow of sheer love for the whole thing, its radiance spilling out from the rink and into the bleachers where it warmed the hearts of those who watched. When the camera panned round this time, all were smiling and leaning forward with delight like children at the circus—they'd fallen in love with him. He skated with grace, skill, and ease, and he happened to win the silver medal. The moral of this story is *not:*

If you love your work,

And you love your audience too,

then you will win a medal

or at least a good review

(no matter how mediocre the acting or miserable the script).

No, there is no moral. Only a reminder.

Exercise: Setting the Tone, Opening the Heart

When preparing to go onstage, there is not always time or stillness available for lengthy exercises, even when you're the only actor in the dressing room. But just five or ten minutes of preparation to clear and open your field and your heart sets a powerful base note for the evening.

Most of this exercise comes from what appears elsewhere in the book; you shift your intention while doing it to suit the needs of moving into performance.

- Begin, as always, by centering and grounding, rooting firmly into the earth's pulse which is going to be carrying you through from beginning to end.
- Know what you want to achieve in this performance and why, and set your intention (see exercise in Chapter 2). It may have to do with being true to a person, a people, a place, and with honoring their lives and endurance. It may have to do with a particular question in your heart about our human story and our world and your intending to be strong enough to ask it in this form. It may have to do with the nature of your relationship to this audience or with the integrity and generosity of your performance at this time. It may be all of the above, or countless other things that remind you of and re-root you in this work of gathering sparks that you have taken on.
- After setting your intention, open your heart chakra and the fourth level of your field. Follow the first half of the exercise for "Building a Listening House" in Chapter 4. Let all that you do in the evening, no matter how bitter or ragged the story, be offered through your heart—both from within the fourth chakra and the fourth level of the field.
- If you are strong enough for it, open as well to the sixth level of the field, expanding your subtle body beyond personal ego to the vibration of unconditional love (see Chapter 3). Tune first, through your imagination, attention, and intention, to the sixth chakra, and from charging and opening that center, move into the sixth level, expanding your field to at least two and one-half feet beyond your

body and sensing the waves of rainbow-colored light tinged by mother-of-pearl moving through it.

- Staying expanded, reaffirm your intention.
- Then (very important!) check that you're still rooted and not wafting out there on an iridescent cloud.

It may be that you do not do every one of the above steps, but find the two or three that offer you just the clarity and strength you need to go on. So be it. I've given you a little more than you may need, so you have something to choose from and make entirely your own. Add to it what you wish—a prayer, a few wise words that grant you openness and courage, a summoning of the spirits of those you are portraying, an image that grants you fire and coherence, a joke that gets you laughing at the bizarre twists of life.

It's best to do the above exercise after you have moved into the subtle body configurations of your character. Yes, you can hold both at once. As you get into costume and stage makeup, bring in the energies of your character. If you will be playing multiple characters during the performance, tune to the field of just the first one, with the assumption that you have rehearsed well the shifting from one to the others. This character may herself not be grounded or centered or open of heart. So be it. Move into that music just as it is until it's firm within you, and a few minutes before the performance begins, move your own field into its centered, rooted, expanded, and heart-charged state, *embracing* the field of the character.

In solo acting, you may find yourself even more sensitive than usual to the varied energies coming toward you from an audience. We learn to ride their waves. It's all we've got, there being no one else on stage with us, and sometimes we become hyper-alert to the force field evolving. It's important, however, not to *interpret* what you're perceiving too quickly, because as in sensing any field, you may know what you perceive but not know what it signifies, and in this case, we run the risk of our wild interpretations affecting the performance.

Years ago, I was touring Frederick Wiseman's monologue *Life and Fate*,[2] the story of a Ukrainian Jewish woman during World War II who smuggles letters to her son from inside a Jewish ghetto where she

---

[2]Adapted from a chapter in Vasily Grossman's novel of that name, now a French film called *The Letter*.

knows that all there will be sent to their deaths within months. She writes these letters with an acute, compassionate, and intelligent eye for the daily lives of the ghetto community in the weeks before their execution, etching in words the mundane and peculiar details of their avoidance or acceptance of their fate. One night I was performing in an old synagogue. Before the show, the director had told me that the pews were packed to overflowing, but I would never have known it from the stage—the lights were such that I could see nothing out there, not even the silhouettes of the audience. All was black. About halfway through the hour-long piece I decided that the director had lied and that no one was in the audience at all, because I could feel nothing from them: no energy, no breath, no sound, no response, no impulse, nothing! The visual blackness was matched by an energetic void. Either no one was there, or if they were, they couldn't connect to this piece and had left in spirit, or maybe I was such a miserable failure they'd fallen asleep in disgust. It was a theatre nightmare, performing for no one and nothing.

At the play's end the applause was delayed and muted, but it told me that at least a few human beings were actually beyond the glare of the lights. I went down to the dressing room in puzzled gloom. After a while, the director came in and said there were some audience members to see me.

"I don't want to see anybody. It was awful. They hated it!" (An embarrassment of ego and self-involvement.)

"Oh be quiet," she said, and opened the dressing room door.

There was a line of elderly people stretched down the hall and up the backstage stairs, people with gray hair and white hair and walking sticks and bent backs, waiting quietly. They came inside in twos and threes and held my hands or patted my cheek. "We were there in that war. We survived. We remember. Thank you for keeping the story alive." And they would turn and go, and the next set would come and take my hands and say "I was there in hell too," or say nothing at all but look at the floor for a moment, tears brimming, and leave. Finally, I said to one woman, "I don't understand. I couldn't hear anything from the audience. I didn't know if you were there." She smiled. "Oh my dear," she said, "that was the sound of our holding our breaths."

It is not our business or within our scope to plan, manipulate, control, or otherwise oversee the nature of an invisible force field arising among us at a given performance. It is ours only to plant the seed with the story; whatever blossoms will come from the sunlight and moisture of lives, spirit, and wonders beyond what we know or carried in with us. Our task at this moment, after all we have gathered, crafted, and rehearsed, is—on one level—to *surrender* to those larger forces and, having made a container for their coming together, to pray only that their mingling be life-giving and transformative.

When we walk another's walk, sing another's melody, swim inside another being's current while holding to the truth, fullness, and failures of our own, we edge a little further toward our communal soul, hoping to catch both the solace and the rough itch of how our stories inter-weave with one another. And as we walk onto the stage, we walk straight into the unknown (who ever knows what will happen?): a smaller unknown than that huge one we're all walking through today, but one we can be thankful for as it gives us a little practice for the big one. Within that space, when the most beautiful song in the world is spoken and heard with enough courage and heart, it may rise like smoke to another kind of ear, and then a kind of miracle can happen, the subtle dance of our common spirit somehow rekindled, revitalized, and transformed in a manner that none of us could have come to all alone.

> Physical energy is diminished by use. Once used, we are left with life-less matter and waste products that are often dangerous to the life process. In contrast, psychic energies are all increased by the numbers of those who participate in their activity. Material things are diminished as more people share them and non-material realities are enhanced as more people share them.[3]

[Enter Rose Solomon, again, to close with one more story.]

ROSE

So one time the Baal Shem Tov chooses one of his disciples, a guy by the name of Wolf, to give to him the great honor of teaching to him all the secret mysti-cal teachings that go with the notes that you blow on the shofar. Now what that is, the shofar. That's the horn of a ram, you see, a ram's horn, and the Jew-ish people, they blow this horn to bring in the holy New Year. And it was said that if you knew all the secret mystical meanings to each and every note that you blow, the sounds would go all the way up to the Holy direct, and they would take with them the prayers of the people.

---

[3]Berry, Thomas. 1999. *The Great Work*. New York: Bell Tower. p. 171.

Well, this guy Wolf was so excited, he was so honored to be given this task that he studied for a whole year. He learned all the secret meanings, he practiced them with the notes, he memorized it in his head; he had it down pat. So comes the New Year, he goes with his horn in front of his whole community of people, their eyes are big with hope and expectation, his heart is pounding away in his chest. He lifts his horn to his lips, and what happens? All the secret mystical meanings go flying right out of his head! He forgets them! He goes searching frantically all around his brain, he can't find one. Whoop! They're gone.

Well, this poor man is so filled with anguish, with pure grief, that he has failed his people, and he can't get their prayers to God, that his heart breaks completely in two. He lifts his horn to his lips, he forgets all about these secret mystical meanings, he does all that is left to him—he blows through the crack in his broken heart.

And what people said: At that moment, heaven and earth came and met each other in the same place, for he had found the way to the Holy.

Our theatre will never capture our whole story, or sing all the strains of our song, or be able to catch and label the unfathomable, unnamable, invisible, and enigmatic soul we crave so much to probe and comprehend. But still we must try and—following our ancient mandate—sing of that soul a hundred million times in a hundred million ways straight through the cracks in our hearts. And once in a while, there will indeed come those shimmering moments, unmeasurable though they be, when we will be caught together inside a taste, a glimmer, a whiff of its sparked and miraculous presence, and our broken hearts will be strengthened.

A FEW BOOKS FOR FURTHER
READING ABOUT SUBTLE ENERGIES

Brennan, Barbara Ann. 1988. *Hands of Light: A Guide to Healing Through the Human Energy Field*. New York: Bantam.

———. 1993. *Light Emerging: The Journey of Personal Healing*. New York: Bantam.

Bruyere, Rosalyn. *Wheels of Light*. Canada: Simon & Schuster.

Goldner, Diane. 1999. *Infinite Grace: Where the Worlds of Science and Spiritual Healing Meet*. Charlottesville, VA: Hampton Roads.

Judith, Anodea. 1992. *Wheels of Life*. St. Paul, MN: Llewellyn Publications.

Judith, Anodea, and Vega, Selene. 1993. *The Sevenfold Journey*. Freedom, CA: The Crossing Press.

Schwarz, Jack. 1980. *Human Energy Systems*. New York: E. P. Dutton.

Talbot, Michael. 1991. *The Holographic Universe*. New York: HarperCollins.